make me
whole

make me whole

An in-depth study through the scriptures on inner healing and wholeness

Joan James

WELCH PUBLISHING COMPANY INC.
Burlington, Ontario, Canada

First Printing 1979
Second Printing 1980
Third Printing 1981
Fourth Printing 1983
Fifth Printing 1984
Sixth Printing 1985
Seventh Printing 1987

Chinese translation 1986

ISBN: 1-55011-040-3

© 1979 by Joan James

Welch Publishing Company Inc.
960 The Gateway
Burlington, Ontario
L7L 5K7 Canada

Printed in Canada

To my husband
LLOYD
who patiently endured the long hours
of my writing, and whose constant
encouragement helped me to bring this
book to its final completion.

CONTENTS

ACKNOWLEDGEMENTS

TO NITA SNYDER who encouraged me to get started, who spent many hours typing and retyping the manuscript, and whose great enthusiasm kept me on target. Her prayers supported me at all times.

TO BEA DAWSON who compiled the notes from my tapes, a most significant task, and helped me put it all together.

TO REV. ALLON HORNBY, my Pastor, who edited the manuscript and gave me most valuable counsel.

TO ALL MY FRIENDS from seminars near and far who have requested this book and encouraged me to write it. I thank you all from my heart.

— Joan James

FOREWORD

Many times people go to their doctors for help when their need is for the "inner healing" as presented in this book by Joan James. Often I have tried to help such people, and I am so glad the Lord led me to Joan.

Since hearing her speak and minister to so many in great need, I have frequently suggested to those searching for help that they attend the series of lectures on which this book is based. Many have been wonderfully touched by the Holy Spirit — the only One who can heal and erase hurts suffered in the process of growing up.

Joan's ministry is indeed precious. Her medical background is useful, but it is her deep knowledge of and dependence on the Word of God which, I believe, makes her such an effective vehicle for God's healing.

This book will be the means of bringing her message of hope to many more than at present, and it will serve as a reference for those of us familiar with her lectures. I shall make sure I have it available in my office.

M. F. Davison, M.D.
925 West Georgia
Vancouver, B.C.

PREFACE

As a pastor I am very aware that "inner healing" is a real need in the lives of many people.

God has given Joan a special ministry in this area. I have time and again seen definite healings in members of our church as Joan has counselled with them. I thank God that she is a loyal and diligent part of our church family and a real support to me as her pastor.

It has been exciting to see the new areas of ministry that God has opened up to Joan these past few years as she has allowed the Holy Spirit to guide her. This book, a new area of ministry, gives the core of her seminar teaching and as such offers significant help to many people. It is practical, Biblical and very readable, and it is a pleasure to recommend it to you.

Allon E. Hornby, Pastor
Broadway Tabernacle
2677 East Broadway
Vancouver, B.C.

INTRODUCTION

"Tell me about yourself," the psychiatrist said to the young man seated before him. Then skilfully probing and prompting, he brought out from the past the traumatic experiences of childhood which had been buried but never resolved. With each poignant memory the patient winced as though reliving all the hurt again. At times his features contorted in anger, and occasionally he wept.

I was sitting in an observation room, unknown to the patient, in a workshop in counselling techniques for nurses at a teaching hospital. We had been studying intensively the reaction of childhood experiences on adult behaviour. Now we were expectantly awaiting some answers. What do you do with the information when you get it all out into the open? I needed to know. I had personality conflicts of my own with which I couldn't cope. I sat on the edge of my seat in anticipation. After the hour-long interview the doctor rose to his feet dismissing the young man with: "Come back and see me in two weeks. In the meantime, here is a prescription for some pills." It was as though he had gathered up all the dirty laundry which he had so methodically spread out to view, put it in a sack and handed it back to the patient. My heart sank.

"My God," I prayed, "there has to be a better solution than this!"

I respect the medical profession most highly — I am part of it. The psychiatrist today is faced with a mammoth problem. The 1974 statistics I received from a large Canadian hospital showed that nearly fifty percent of hospital beds were occupied by psychiatric cases. In recent years, however, these have been reduced by the use of other mental health facilities in the community. Many psychiatrists realize that their best treatment is only palliative.

Through many years as a registered nurse I was often projected into a counselling situation, and particularly so in the last ten years of my nursing career where I served in Occupational Health. Many and varied were the problems in interpersonal relationships in the work force. Add to these, hostilities in marital and/or parental relationships in the home and the stress reaches a breaking point. Through three years of voluntary counselling in a girls' detention centre I was brought face to face with the tragic consequences of breakdown in the home, a drug-oriented and permissive society, and a generation without roots. Yes, we were able to help — to a degree, but I wasn't satisfied with a cover up. I knew people who had been on tranquilizers for more than ten years. Somewhere we were

1

failing them. Is this what life is all about? The question nagged continually at my heart.

In 1970 I retired from professional nursing and began to earnestly seek the Lord for *His* answers. As I look back now, I see how graciously He brought about a chain of circumstances which brought me into His beautiful plan.

It started like this: Our church choir was invited to give a Gospel concert in a Catholic service one Sunday evening. Our director ad-libbed his introduction by saying, "Maybe you thought this was a youth group, but as you see we have Mama bears, Papa bears and Baby bears. I would like you to meet one of the Mama bears." Being used to his ability to improvise, I was not surprised when he called me out to give a few words of greeting and testimony. Gladly I told of the reality of Jesus Christ in my life.

Later, while I was enjoying fellowship with some of the people, a nun rushed up to me, grasped both my hands and said, "Mama Bear, whatever it is you have, I must have it too. I'm sure this is what I have been searching for in the last ten years." (I realized at that moment that she didn't even know my name.)

"Do you know the Holy Spirit?" I asked her.

She quickly replied, "I have been reading everything about Him that I can get my hands on."

"The Holy Spirit is the One Who makes Jesus real to us," I explained, "and Who permeates our lives with that reality." I then recommended that she go into the little chapel to be alone with the Lord. I said, "Open your life to Him. Ask him to come in and fill your being with Himself. Tucked up in your head is all the knowledge *about* Him, but you need to *know* Him in reality."

A few days later she phoned me, and the ring in her voice told me she had a new song in her heart. "Joan, will you come to the convent and have lunch with us?" she said. "I want to introduce you to the other nuns."

"I would love to," I told her.

This was to be a totally new experience for me. My association with Catholics up to this point had been limited to the choir concert and my first year of formal education in Grade One in a Catholic school. At that time my mother undoubtedly had hoped to make a lady out of her tomboy daughter through this type of schooling; however, I'm afraid she conceded failure after that one year. My strongest memory of that time is the aura of mysticism which surrounded the nuns and the curiosity they provoked in my childish mind. Some of my little friends and I learned that they slept in their individual classrooms. It was our greatest desire to peek through the door early some morning and discover what they wore under those long black habits! Of course we never succeeded, and I grew up with some very strange misconceptions.

Now as I approached my luncheon engagement, my mind was filled with conjecture. The picture I had formulated in my imagination simply disappeared as we sat around the table and shared the love of Jesus in the

2

most beautiful harmony of fellowship. There were five of us — four nuns and myself, and the barriers fell away in the warmth of the Spirit.

This was to be a memorable day for even another reason: It was then I met the nun whom God was to use in a very specific way in my life. Her name was Sr. Margaret Toner. She was engaged in mission work in Peru and had come to Canada for a short time of special study in university. There was that unmistakable radiance of the Holy Spirit about her, which prompted me to ask her, "Sister Margaret, will you tell me how you came into the Life in the Spirit?"

"Have you got three hours?" she laughingly answered.

"I've got all the time it takes," I responded.

She then proceeded to tell me an amazing story. The wind of the Spirit had breathed in renewal in the convent in Peru. Those who entered in were transformed — their lives were filled with radiant joy. Margaret was awed, but she watched from a distance — afraid, and yet longing to participate. Finally one night she decided to attend their charismatic prayer group. She sat right at the back so she could get out in a hurry if it was too much for her. But she stayed through the whole meeting, strangely drawn by something she couldn't quite define. She continued to go, each time getting just a little closer until she said, "I had to touch this for myself."

One evening she went forward for prayer. The priest laid his hands on her, and she waited but nothing happened. She felt all tied up inside. The release she longed for didn't come. A great heaviness seemed to be upon her. The priest, being very sensitive to the Spirit, suggested that this could be the result of something that had happened in her childhood. He said, "We will ask the Lord Jesus to walk back with us through the years and show us what has caused such bondage."

As they waited before the Lord, a hidden memory began to stir in her mind. It was something that she did not consciously remember, but she had been told about it as a child and had forgotten over the years. She then began to recount the story: "When my mother was carrying me in the womb, there were three tragic deaths in the family that followed one right after the other. When I was born, my mother was in deep depression. I was born in the midst of this great sorrow and melancholy."

The priest then simply said, "This may be it. Let us ask the Lord Jesus to heal even the memory of that thing, to heal your subconscious mind where it is imprinted, and to release you completely." And so he prayed.

"Immediately I felt something like a bubble rising from the depths of my being," she said, "until it burst from my lips in worship and praise in a language which I had never learned — it was the language of the Spirit." Since that day she had walked in a whole new life with Jesus. She added, "I received an inner healing."

Those two words — *inner healing* — suddenly became alive to me. I had never heard them used before. And there came to my heart a sense of destiny — a feeling that I was standing on the threshold of God's unfolding of His plan for my life.

3

One morning, very soon after, I knelt by the big chair in my living room. I said, "Lord, I must know the reality of 'inner healing' in my own life, for my own conflicts. I must meet You *now*; otherwise I cannot go on."

You see, for years I had lived behind a mask. Underneath was a devastating inferiority complex. Only my husband knew. He would hear me dragging myself in the dust, berating and blaming myself, and he would say, "Honey, you've got to get over it." But I didn't know how, so I would put on the mask again and play the game of pretend. My Christian life was up and down like a yo-yo. I was tired of living this way.

I was desperately serious with God that day. I knew I must stay on my knees until He showed me the root of my problem. Walking back through my life, I waited and memory began to stir. I saw a little girl — myself — and an experience from which I instantly recoiled. I saw my fear and the attempts to hide it. And so I buried it unresolved. But down through the years it burrowed into my self-image, undermining and destroying. I didn't know until this moment of illumination by the Holy Spirit.

"Oh, God," I cried, "don't let me bury it again. Heal me, in the Name of Jesus, of every memory until not even a scar remains." As I waited weeping in His Presence, something began to happen. It was as though I was washed through and through, then bathed in healing oil. Great joy filled me. I knew that thing could never plague me again. I was free — free to be me! And then another awareness burst in upon me — inner healing is real.

There was still a further step for me to take — one in which I would need help in prayer. I had had coronary heart disease. The doctor's diagnosis was: "Myocardial insufficiency due to coronary atherosclerosis." For two years I was maintained on an anti-coagulant drug. I often suffered severe angina and always kept the nitroglycerin handy. God had graciously healed me of this condition, and yet there seemed to hang over me an oppression. I hadn't told anyone, not even my husband. Somehow it seemed too vague. But it was always there. I could make no plans for even a year ahead. I knew my life span was limited. I began to expect with every exertion that this would be it — I would collapse and die.

One day Sister Margaret came to have lunch with me. She would be returning to Peru very soon. Suddenly I thought, "I can tell *her*. She will understand." With her beautiful insight she put her hands on my shoulders and began to pray, first of all in her prayer language in the Spirit, then in English. As she did, I realized that God had given her a deeper understanding of my fear than I had told her. Her prayer was simple and gentle, yet full of faith. I felt a rest come over me. That was all.

Several days later, I was digging industriously in the garden. Previously, with each shovelful of earth, I would be expecting to be lying dead on the ground. But something was different now. The oppression was gone! I rushed in to the phone and dialed Margaret. "I'm healed, I'm healed," I cried. "I'm strong. I'm well. I'm going to live." Once again a great joy surged through my soul. Then I knew that God had a plan for my life — to bring His healing to others. I didn't know how, but I started to search His Word with an intense and insatiable hunger.

Scarcely realizing what was happening, I found myself becoming deeply involved in a program of personal counselling. People came from all walks of life — the younger and the older. Their problems were multiple and varied: depression, anger, guilt and fear. Some were bound by alcohol or drugs; others were slaves to sexual passions or deviations. All were in desperate need. As we worked together applying the principles God was teaching me through His Word, things began to happen. Jesus stepped into these lives in miracles of deliverance and healing.

One day my husband said, "Honey, it seems like our house is always full of people. What will we do about it?" I knew what he said was true. There was no way we could continue to minister on an individual basis. There were just too many crying for help. As I laid it before the Lord in earnest prayer, a thought came to me: "Maybe I could counsel the people in groups." I said, "Lord, if this is from You, will You open the door?" In a very short time I was approached by someone who asked me if I would be willing to give a workshop in this type of counselling ministry at a retreat. My response was an immediate "yes." I knew this was God's provision.

After repeating this workshop at several retreats, I began to feel an urge to expand the ministry. It seemed that I was only giving the bare kernel of truth and much more was needed. Again I put it before the Lord — I told no one. God works in marvellous ways: He sent the same person as before to ask me to consider giving a series of classes to some women's home Bible Study groups. I guess my mouth fell open in amazement as I simply gasped "yes" again. I had only the workshop material prepared at that time, but as I taught the series, the Holy Spirit brought to my remembrance the principles *He* had taught me over the four years of personal counselling. In this way I wrote them lesson by lesson.

One day I heard the women remarking, "Our husbands also need this message. What can we do about getting them into it?"

I said, "Why don't you pray?" They did. I prayed too — "Lord, I'm willing to go wherever You open the door." And so the invitations started to come to minister in churches across the land, and we have gone in obedience to His call, my husband and I together.

And now in response to the many requests of those to whom we have ministered, and because of the urgency in our own hearts, we present this book. It is an in-depth study of the truths of Inner Healing as the Holy Spirit has taught me over the last seven years of counselling, individually and in seminars. My heart's prayer is that God will use it to bring His healing to multitudes, and to you.

We have used many illustrations and all are true. However, we have changed the names to protect the people involved. None of these stories are singular — they are repeated over and over in the varying circumstances of life.

CHAPTER ONE

FINDING THE REAL "YOU"

"He sent His word and healed them, and delivered them from their destructions" (Ps. 107:20).

The principles taught in this book are based upon the Scriptures. I am not offering psychiatry nor psychology — these have their place and I respect them. In a TV interview I was asked the question, "Why do you use the Bible in your ministry of counselling?" My answer was, "Because it is the only textbook in which I have found the answers." I heard a similar answer given by a psychiatrist in a televised interview. He stated that the Bible is still the best textbook on psychiatry. In the January 1976 issue of Moody Monthly there appeared an article written by Dr. Malcolm Beck, a former president of the Canadian Psychiatric Association. He stated that orthodox, supernatural Christianity has more to teach psychiatry than psychiatry has to teach the churches. He concluded that the majority of his patients would not need to see him if they had deep religious convictions.

Our minds today are under a constant barrage of negatives hurled at us from the television screen, the news media, the educational system, and even our everyday conversation. We are programmed to think sickness, violence and despair. Our only defense is to re-program our minds with the positive absolutes of God's Word. This Word is forever settled in heaven according to Psalm 119:89. It does not fluctuate with the changing social mores of any people, nor with the social customs. It is a universal Word — "God so loved *the world* . . .", not just a segment of it.

The writer to the Hebrews tells us that He Who created the worlds upholds, maintains, guides and propels the universe by the Word of His power (Heb. 1:1-3). Space programs were set according to the absolutes on which our solar system operates, and the United States successfully landed a man on the moon. If God had been capricious — if He had tipped the axis of this planet the barest fraction, they would never have reached their target. But God's Word is absolute — with Him there is not even a "shadow of turning" (James 1:17).

In his book *"He is There and He is Not Silent"* Dr. Francis Schaeffer tells us that reading the Bible every day of one's life gives one a different mentality. He says, "Do not minimize the fact that in reading the Bible we are living in a mentality which is the right one opposed to the great wall of

7

the other mentality which is forced upon us from every side — in education, in literature, in the arts, and in the mass media" (P. 78). Therefore, without apology, I bring this teaching of inner healing to you that through the eternal Word of God your faith and experience may stand on solid ground.

I have entitled this chapter "Finding the Real You" because we must discover what it means to be a whole person. For too long our ills have been treated in parts as though we could be dissected and spread around here and there. The medical doctor has been concerned only with the physical, the psychiatrist with the emotional, and the pastor or minister with the spiritual. But we are not fragmented persons — we are a composite unity.

As I read in Acts 9:34 where Peter said to AEneas, "Jesus Christ maketh thee *whole,*" and in Mark 6:56 that "as many as touched Him were made *whole,*" I searched for the meaning of "wholeness". As I prayerfully studied, my attention was captivated by the words of Jesus recorded in Mark 12:30-31:

> "And thou shalt love the Lord thy God with all thy heart, and with all thy soul, and with all thy mind, and with all thy strength: this is the first commandment.
> And the second is like, namely this, thou shalt love thy neighbour as thyself. There is none other commandment greater than these."

I had known and memorized these verses many years ago, but now these words seemed to stand out in bold relief: *heart, soul, mind, strength* and *neighbour.* They seemed to fall into a pattern forming a complete unity as indicated in the diagram.

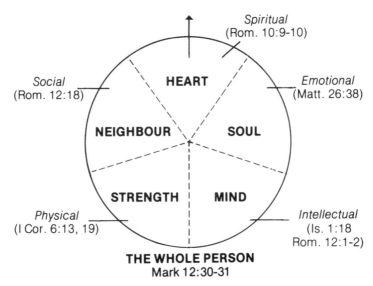

THE WHOLE PERSON
Mark 12:30-31

THE HEART

What is this area to which Jesus refers? Is it that muscular organ lying within the human breast which pumps life-giving blood throughout the body? No. It is even more vital than that. It is the spiritual dimension of man's being which by faith touches God and receives His life-giving Spirit. Paul tells us that "the word of faith" is not only in our mouth but also in our *heart*. He says that "if you confess with your mouth 'Jesus is Lord', and believe in your *heart* that God raised Him from the dead, you will be saved. For it is with your *heart* that you believe and are justified...." (Rom. 10:9-10 N.I.V.) It is the channel through which you exercise faith:

"Trust in the Lord with all thine *heart*" (Prov. 3:5),

and also through which you exercise worship:

"I will praise thee with my whole *heart*" (Ps. 9:1).

The channel must be open and clean:

"Blessed are the pure in *heart;* for they shall see God" (Matt. 5:8).

We must guard it well:

"Keep thine heart with all diligence for out of it are the issues (or springs) of life" (Prov. 4:23).

THE SOUL

The word is translated from the Greek "psyche" from which our word "psychiatry" is derived. It is the emotional area of our beings — the ego, the "me", where I hurt and feel. Jesus said:

"My *soul* is exceeding sorrowful, even unto death" (Matt. 26:38).

How deep and intense was His suffering as

"He bore our griefs and carried our sorrows" (Is. 53:4).

The Psalmist asked:

"Why art thou cast down, O my *soul?* and why art thou disquieted within me?" (Ps. 43:5).

There are also emotions of joy:

"My *soul* shall be joyful in the Lord, and in His salvation" (Ps. 35:9),

and love:

"I found Him whom my soul loveth; I held Him and would not let Him go" (S. of S. 3:4).

I wrote this verse in the flyleaf of my Bible when I was fourteen years of age, for it was then that Jesus stepped into the darkness and despair of my life and gave me a reason for living. I was lying on my bed, afraid and alone, and He came to me in a vision. I gave Him my heart that night, and words can never express the joy I have known walking with Him down through these many years.

THE MIND

The intellectual area of our being. God has given to us the capacity for knowledge and reason. He does not put a premium on ignorance. Christianity is a matter of faith, but faith is not divorced from reason. As I once heard Dr. Schaeffer say — "Faith is not a blind leap in the dark." It is based upon the eternal absolutes of God's Word as imprinted upon the mind through reading and hearing.

God calls us to put our minds into action in the words of Isaiah 1:18:

"Come now and let us *reason* together, saith the Lord: though your sins be as scarlet, they shall be as white as snow...."

In Romans 12:1 Paul beseeches us in view of all God's great mercies toward us that we make a decisive dedication to Him of all our faculties, which is our "*reasonable* (or rational and intelligent) service."

Some have told us that because Christianity is a matter of faith, apologetics is not necessary. However, the Bible states in I Peter 3:15:

"Always be ready to give a logical defense to any one who asks you to account for the hope that is in you, but do it courteously and respectfully." (Amplified Bible).

God wants to:

"imprint His laws upon our hearts and inscribe them on our *minds*" (Heb. 10:16 Amp).

And Peter says to

"gird up the loins of your mind" (I Pet. 1:13).

Or, in other words, "Get ready for action!"

THE STRENGTH

This is the physical — the body. I have heard some folks say, "It doesn't matter — it's my body — I can do with it as I please." But this is not so for the Christian. He is governed by "the law of the Spirit of life in Christ Jesus" (Rom. 8:2). He is no longer his own to do his own thing. I would like to quote I Corinthians 6:19-20 in full from the Amplified Bible:

"Do you not know that your *body* is the temple — the very sanctuary — of the Holy Spirit Who lives within you, Whom you have received (as a Gift) from God?

You are not your own,
You were bought for a price — purchased with a preciousness and paid for, made His own. So then, honor God and bring glory to Him in your *body.*"

As a Christian, your body now belongs to Christ with the sole purpose of glorifying Him. If you abuse your body through the indulgence of its fleshly appetites, you abuse the temple of the Holy Spirit. In our permissive society God has not left us without direction: Paul states very clearly and succinctly in this regard —

"The body is not meant for sexual immorality, but for the Lord, and the Lord for the body" (I Cor. 6:13 N.I.V.).

This is not an arbitrary decision on God's part. Paul goes on in this passage of Scripture to explain: sexual immorality is totally destructive to the person and to his relationship to Christ. Neither is it only the sexual drives which must be disciplined, but again Paul states clearly:

"Whether you eat or drink or whatever you do, do all for the glory of God" (I Cor. 10:31).

This is an all-inclusive injunction referring to every activity of this physical body.

THE NEIGHBOUR

This is the area of our social relationships. I guess the question is still being asked, "Who is my neighbour?" And the answer is just as straightforward now as it was when recorded by Luke in his Gospel — it is any fellow human being. And the one who was "a neighbour" was the one who "showed mercy."

The social dimension is an integral part of the whole person. The state of these horizontal relationships is vitally important, and great emphasis is placed on this throughout the Scriptures. Sometimes people try to isolate themselves among little groups of like people with whom they feel comfortable, but sooner or later they are going to have to mingle with the crowd. Such was my young friend, Nancy.

Nancy had her first job, and she needed it because she now had her own apartment and a car to operate. The trouble was that she hated everyone in the office. There wasn't one person she could get along with. She wanted to quit — surely she could find a better bunch than this office had to offer. But jobs weren't that easy to find. What should she do? This was her continual woeful lament. Finally one day I said to her, "You know, it's a funny thing but it doesn't matter where you go or what job you get, you're still going to have to work with people. There's really nothing else on this planet to work with. So you might as well make up your mind now that you're going to make the best of it."

There is a secret, and it is found tucked away in this verse found in Romans 12:18:

"If it be possible, as much as lieth in you, live peaceably with all men."

Notice that there is no discrimination here — the classification is "all men", not just those people to whom we relate well. Now the secret lies in that little phrase "as much as lieth in you." It is upon this that the possibility of living peaceably with all men depends.

Have you ever heard someone say, seemingly with great pride, "I gave him a piece of my mind!"? The question is: "Whose mind are you giving away?" If it is your own, then you should be careful how much you give away — you may find yourself shortchanged one day. However, if you "have the mind of Christ," you have sufficient and to spare, for His mind is renewed in you day by day (II Corinthians 4:16).

"Let this *mind* be *in you* which was also in Christ Jesus: Who . . . took upon Himself the form of a servant. . . Who humbled Himself. . ." (Phil. 2:5, 7-8).

Yes, this is the secret — the Spirit of Christ dwelling in you.

Jesus commanded that we should love the Lord our God with all our heart, soul, mind, strength and our neighbour as ourselves. He did not set aside one area as unimportant or without meaning. These five dimensions constitute the whole person. We are not just physical beings, nor just intellectual, but we are these *plus* the spiritual, emotional and social, which all together form a composite unity. There are no clearly defined lines of separation as shown on the diagram (which is merely an aid to clarify the understanding of our basic selves.) We cannot cut ourselves into pieces like a pie and place one piece here and another somewhere else.

Unfortunately, this is what we have tried to do. We have segregated the spiritual in a little box which we call "church", and the emotional we have reserved for such things as our favorite sports event when the home team wins. Similarly, we have set aside the others in what we thought were tight compartments, until we have become fragmented persons with nothing to bind us together again.

What we have failed to understand is that each area of our beings is an integral part of the whole, flowing and blending like the colors of a rainbow. We are like a symphony — if one instrument is out of tune, it throws out the harmony of the whole. Whatever takes place in any one of these areas inevitably affects the whole.

We are indeed complex beings "fearfully and wonderfully made", as the Psalmist has declared. In the Living Bible the thought is paraphrased this way:

"You made all the delicate, inner parts of my body, and knit them together in my mother's womb. Thank You for making me so wonderfully complex!" (Ps. 139:13-14).

Solomon made a terse statement concerning man when he said: "As he thinks...so is he" (Prov. 23:7). It is an awesome thing to consider that what we think, what we process into our minds will determine our actions, our relationships to others and to God, and the state of our emotions.

I watched on the TV news one day a gigantic sea of mud loosened from a mountainside and slowly invading a village below. It seemed like the tentacles of some monster reaching out in every direction in destruction. Likewise, while travelling through a fertile cultivated valley, I have seen the irrigation canals weaving through the fields giving life and succulence to the crops.

The lesson we can learn from these two stories is apparent: that which enters our lives can be a destructive force or a life-giving stream. The difference is that *we* have a choice. The person who chooses to be ruled by negative emotions such as hatred, bitterness or self pity will inevitably reap the harvest in his body. Psychosomatic illness has become such a perplexing problem to the medical profession that many doctors are realizing the need to return to what they term as "wholistic medicine."

A most pertinent illustration of the inseparability of the five dimensions of the being of man is found recorded in the book of Genesis. Adam and Eve were in perfect harmony with their Father God and with one another. They walked together with Him in a beautiful communion. We are not told how long this continued, but one day something happened. They chose to disobey the one restriction placed upon them when God said, "Of the tree of the knowledge of good and evil, thou shalt not eat..." And that precious relationship was broken.

How did it all begin? Satan (the serpent) planted a question mark in Eve's mind — "Hath God said?" Then Eve made her first mistake — she dialogued with Satan. Instead of casting it from her as a horrendous thought, she held it and mulled it over in her mind. Then one day while walking in the garden, she stopped by the "tree" just to look. It seemed so pleasant and lovely. She reached out to the fruit to feel its beautiful texture and to smell its fragrance.

"Surely this would be good food," she thought, "and besides that, it could make one wise." Grasping it in her hands, she took one delicious bite. "M-m-m, it's luscious, Adam," she said. "Here, have some," and she handed it to her husband who, the Bible says, was "with her" and he also ate of it.

As they were munching away, suddenly they looked at one another. Something was different — they had never felt this way before. But now they were ashamed of their naked bodies, and they tried to hide themselves from one another's eyes. Oh, what would they do? Taking fig leaves, they fashioned them into aprons to cover themselves, and scarcely were they finished when evening fell, and they heard the Voice of God as He came to walk with them.

But now their response to the beloved Voice was only guilt, and running, they hid themselves among the trees. Still His Voice came searching and calling, "Adam, where are you?" It seemed to echo from tree to tree — it was everywhere, inescapable.

Adam said, "I heard Your Voice, and I was afraid," (guilt always spawns fear) "because I was naked, and I hid myself."

And God said, "Who told you that you were naked? Have you eaten of the tree I commanded you that you should not eat?"

Then Adam blamed the only neighbour he had, his wife: "The woman You gave me," he accused, "she made me do it." So we can see the devastation of the whole person, as I have tried to illustrate graphically in the diagram.

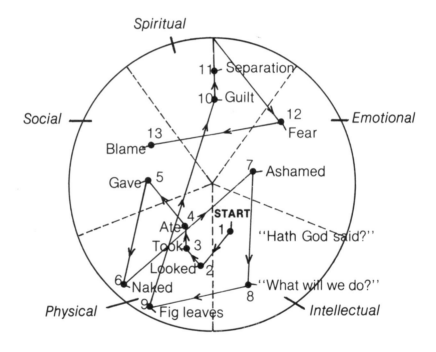

But God did not leave mankind in the hopelessness of despair. He made a blessed provision for the "wholeness" of every person. Into the darkest hour of human history there came the Light, and the angel said to Joseph:

"Thou shalt call His Name Jesus for He shall save His people from their sins" (Matt. 1:21).

Because of this, Peter was able to declare to AEneas so long ago, "Jesus Christ maketh thee whole" (Acts 9:34), and we resound the glorious truth as it has echoed down through the centuries that "Jesus Christ is the same yesterday, and today, and forever" (Heb. 13:8) to all who will hear and believe.

CHAPTER TWO

REACHING FOR YOUR GREATEST POTENTIAL

How can you be what God intends you to be — a whole person? Come with me on a little study of Greek — the original language in which the New Testament was written. Let us consider the word "sōzō" and its English renditions found in the King James Bible. In some instances it is translated "saved" as in

"Believe on the Lord Jesus Christ and thou shalt be *saved*" (Acts 16:31), and

"By grace are ye *saved* through faith; and that not of yourselves: it is the gift of God" (Eph. 2:8).

This same word "sōzō" is also translated "healed" as in Acts 14:9 where Paul perceived that the man who had been a cripple from his mother's womb "had faith to be *healed*". (It is significant to note here Sr. Margaret's healing — she had been crippled emotionally from her mother's womb.)

Then again we find another translation is "whole", as given in Matthew 9:22 where Jesus said to the woman who pressed through the crowd and touched the hem of His garment:

"Daughter, thy faith hath made thee *whole.*"

To blind Bartimaeus Jesus pronounced:

"Go thy way, thy faith hath made thee *whole.*" (Mark 10:52).

And Mark 6:56 concludes with these words:

"As many as touched Him were made *whole.*"

To be "saved" means to be "healed" and to be made "whole". This is the completeness of God's salvation through His Son, the Lord Jesus Christ.

The word "salvation" is translated from the Greek "sōtēria", which literally means *"safety and soundness."* There are two aspects here: when you are "saved" through faith in Jesus Christ, you are truly safe for eternity. Hear the words of Jesus:

"I give unto them eternal life; and they shall never perish, neither shall any man pluck them out of My hand.
My Father, which gave them Me, is greater than all; and no man is

able to pluck them out of My Father's hand" (John 10:28-29).

But what about the "now"? Has God just promised us a "pie in the sky by-and-by" salvation? In the meantime, do you have to hobble through this earthly life as best you can, barely hanging on by the skin of your teeth?

No way! There is a provision for your "today". It is included in the salvation package, and an inseparable part of it. It is *"soundness"*. I would like to illustrate the meaning of this aspect from an experience of my nursing days in the out-patient department of the hospital. After removing a plaster cast from a young lad's leg, the doctor carefully tapped up and down over the fracture area, then reassuringly pronounced: "Perfectly sound!" What did he mean? Simply that the leg was healed — it was whole. The boy could walk and run on it. He could ride his bicycle, engage in sports and do all the normal things ooys like to do. That is "soundness".

There is one place in the King James Bible where the word "sōzō" is translated "preserve" (II Timothy 4:18). I like the Wuest translation which expresses the totality which I want to convey to you: "The Lord will keep me *safe and sound* for His Kingdom...."

The very word "Jesus" in the Hebrew means "salvation". It is "Yeshua". He is not just the best way — He is the *only* way.

"Neither is there salvation (safety and soundness) in any other: for there is none other name under heaven given among men, whereby we must be saved" (Acts 4:12).

"Wholeness" is found uniquely in God's provision of salvation: it is every area of our beings brought under the redemptive work of the Cross of Jesus Christ. The question is: how can this be brought into reality in each individual life? One young man asked me, "How can the death of Jesus Christ on a cross two thousand years ago relate to me today?"

To answer this, first of all, we must understand that Jesus is the *unique* Son of God in the fact of His virgin birth. He is:

"...holy, blameless, unstained by sin, separated from sinners and exalted higher than the heavens" (Heb. 7:26 Amplified).

The Scriptures say:

"As by one man (Adam) sin entered into the world, and death by sin; and so death passed upon all men, for all have sinned" (Rom. 5:12).

Man's blood is subject to death and corruption because of sin. Of all who have ever been born on this earth, Jesus Christ alone had "incorruptible" blood flowing in His veins. He was totally untainted by man's sin.

When studying my obstetrics textbook as a student nurse, I discovered a truth which set my heart leaping in praise to God. The words were these:

> "There is no direct connection between the blood of the fetus and that of the mother; the exchanges of water, oxygen, and food must occur by osmosis."

Jesus Christ was and is indeed the sinless One Whose death alone could atone for my sin, and the sin of all mankind. Therefore, because His Blood is incorruptible, it is still efficacious *today* for our pardon and cleansing, and the Apostle John could say with utmost assurance:

> "If we walk in the light, as He is in the light, we have fellowship one with another, and the Blood of Jesus Christ His Son cleanseth us from all sin" (I John 1:7).

Wuest translates the verb as "continually cleansing". Why? Let me repeat — His Blood is incorruptible. Therefore:

> "When He had by Himself purged our sins, He sat down on the right hand of the majesty on high" (Heb. 1:3).

It is also of vital importance to understand our eternal spirit — the spiritual dimension of our being. In his book *"Surgery of the Soul"* Dr. William Standish Reed notes that there is no way comparable to Christianity which gives honor to the eternal spirit of man or which shows him the means of personal salvation and the way to wholeness and eternal life. It has been said that Christianity is not just an ethical system but the history of the redemption of mankind. The great triumphant song in Heaven is:

> "Thou was slain, and hast redeemed us to God by Thy Blood out of every kindred, and tongue, and people, and nation" (Rev. 5:9).

The Scriptures teach us that *man's spirit is eternal*. In His dying moments on the Cross Jesus said:

> "Father, into Thy hands I commit My spirit" (Luke 23:46).

And as Stephen succumbed to the rocks hurled down upon him by the jeering mob, he looked up to Heaven and said:

> "Lord Jesus, receive my spirit" (Acts 7:59).

As we have previously mentioned, man's spirit is often represented in Scripture by the "heart", and I refer you now to a few more verses which are pertinent:

> "They shall praise the Lord who diligently seek Him and require Him as their greatest need. May your *heart* be quickened *now and forever*" (Psalm 22:26 Amplified).

Psalm 69:32 states that "your *heart* shall *live* that seek God," and Ezekiel 11:19 as given by the Amplified Bible reads:

"And I will give them one heart — a new heart — and I will put a new spirit within them; and I will take the stony (unnaturally hardened) heart out of their flesh, and will give them a heart of flesh (sensitive and responsive to the touch of God)."

As the heart in the physical sense pumps life-giving blood throughout our bodies, so it is through the area of our spirit that the Life of Jesus flows into every part of our beings. Jesus spoke of "a river of living water flowing out of our innermost being" (John 7:38). Every river must have a source, and the headwaters of this river is in Heaven "proceeding out of the throne of God and the Lamb" (Rev. 22:1). Man's spirit is his vital link with the Source. It is through this devotional part of our being which touches God by faith that the river flows, bringing life and wholeness.

There is another analogy given us in Scripture which would be well for us to take note of here.

"The spirit of man is the *lamp* of the Lord, searching all his innermost parts" (Prov. 20:27 Amplified).

In the natural, the human eye receives light and changes it to nerve impulses, which in turn may make muscles move or glands flow. So it is in the spiritual — the spirit of man is the eye which receives the light of God, and this light searches all his being, both revealing and healing.

Jesus enlarges on this thought when He says in Matthew 6:22-23 (and I am paraphrasing this):

"The *light* of the body is the *eye* (or the spirit); if therefore your eye is single (the meaning from the Greek is 'free from defect, sound'), then your entire body (your whole being) will be full of light. But if your eye (or spiritual life) is evil (impure, unsound — you shut out the light), then your whole body shall be full of darkness.... And how great is that darkness!"

It is fear and guilt, torment and terror, hopelessness and worthlessness, frustration, confusion, loneliness and despair.

Knowing all this, man still has a dilemma. Jesus said it is the "pure in heart" who shall see God (Matthew 5:8). But man's heart is not pure. It is "deceitful above all things, and desperately wicked: who can know it?" (Jer. 17:9). According to Ephesians 2:1, man is "dead in trespasses and sins." He cannot grasp nor understand the things of the Spirit of God; they are "foolishness" to him (I Cor. 2:14). Job cried out, "How can mortal man be right before God?" (Job 9:2). Read his despair as he continues:

"For God is not a mere man, as I am, that I should answer Him, that we should come together in court. There is no umpire between us, who might lay His hand upon us both (would that there were!)" (Job 9:32-33).

But there is *now* — His Name is Jesus. He is the Umpire, the "one Mediator between God and man" (I Tim. 2:5). He Who is the Son, co-equal and co-eternal with God, took upon Himself "the form of a servant, and was made in the likeness of men" (Phil. 2:7) that He might lay His hand upon us both and bridge the awful gulf of separation. He has restored the broken lines of communication — He has opened up the channel for the river to flow. He has broken down the hopelessness and made a way for man to come into God's Presence again; and it all happened at the Cross:

"But now in Christ Jesus ye who sometimes were far off are made nigh by the blood of Christ.
For He is our peace...." (Eph. 2:13-14).

Maybe you are thinking, "How can this happen to me? How can I be sure? It all sounds so beautiful, but I'm not a part of it. How can that which seems so dead and unresponsive in me be brought to life?"

These are questions I have been asked, and the answer is decisive and forthright — there has to be a *new birth*. As Jesus told Nicodemus:

"Marvel not — do not be surprised, astonished — at My telling you, you must all be born anew (from above)" (John 3:7 Amplified),

so we too must be born again in order to know and experience the reality of the Kingdom of God. I want to explain the meaning of the new birth in the most simple and practical terms that you may understand with your intellect and be forearmed against Satan's lies (for he will try to steal it from you).

Jesus warned of this when He said:

"When anyone hears the message about the kingdom, and *does not understand* it, the evil one comes and snatches it away" (Matt. 13:19 N.I.V.).

Satan will whisper in your ear, "Don't believe it. It is all imagination — you're just emotionally psyched up!" But when the experience of salvation is grounded on the truths of God's Word, you have a counterattack for Satan which will send Him packing, and you will stand firm, unmoved and unshakable.

Let us return to the conversation Jesus had with Nicodemus where He said:

"That which is born of the flesh is flesh; and that which is born of the Spirit is spirit" (John 3:6).

He is talking here about two births: the physical which comes first and the spiritual which is second. It is another birth. This is clearly stated in I Corinthians 15:46.

19

"The spiritual did not come first, but the natural, and *after that* the spiritual" (N.I.V.)

Each is referred to as a birth, so they must have much in common. Let us look at natural birth first — it is the only way any one of us arrived on this planet! It is thus: the seed of the father unites with the egg of the mother, and by the principle of life (which is in God's hands alone) conception takes place and a new being is born. Jesus always illustrated His truths in understandable human terms, so we can understand spiritual birth by comparing its similarities with the natural.

First, we will consider the spiritual seed which Jesus identified in this succinct statement of fact: "The seed *is* the Word of God" (Luke 8:11). We find it related vitally to the new birth in Peter's words:

"Being born again, not of corruptible *seed,* but of incorruptible (imperishable), by the Word of God, which liveth and abideth forever" (1 Peter 1:23).

This Book we know as the Bible is God's eternal Word to mankind. Down through the centuries it has been banned, bombed, and burned; but no attempts of men nor devils can ever extinguish it — it is "settled forever in Heaven" (Ps. 119:89) and engraved in the hearts of God's people.

Spiritual birth, like natural birth, requires two vital ingredients: the seed and the egg, neither of which can reproduce without the other. You will find the identity of the spiritual "egg" in Hebrews 4:2 which says:

"The Word preached did not profit them, not being mixed with *faith* in them that heard it."

There is in every human heart a little egg of faith which is as natural as breathing. Some people say, "I don't have any faith," and I must quickly affirm, "Yes, you do." The Bible assures us that "God has dealt to every man the measure of faith" (Romans 12:3). You could not exist a day without it — everything you do requires faith, whether eating, drinking, going to bed or rising in the morning. It isn't the size or the amount of faith that is important. Consider the fact that all of our beginnings were from tiny ova (or eggs) that measured approximately 1/125th of an inch in diameter. (Some of us look at ourselves *now* and wonder how that could have been!) The requirement is that it must be alive and it must be activated.

When this happens in the physical, the egg bursts from its little sac in the ovary and proceeds on its way to unite with the implanted seed. In the spiritual, as you hear the Word of God and receive it into your intellect, that little egg of faith in your heart begins to stir and come alive, and you sense a great longing to reach out to touch God and to know Him. This is what has been happening in your heart as you have been hearing His Word in the Scripture passages quoted in the pages of this book — it is a Bible principle at work:

"Faith comes by hearing, and hearing by the Word of God" (Rom. 10:17).

Even now, faith may be seeking to burst from the confines of your heart as something within you cries out for *your* new birth. Perhaps there are words of confession pressing at your lips, but you don't know how to express them. Will you let me help you? May I suggest a prayer for you to pray as you bow before Him now?

"Lord Jesus, I know I am a sinner in need of a Saviour. I believe You are the Son of God, and that You came to earth and died on the Cross to pay the penalty of my sins. I believe God raised You up again, and today You are alive, seated at the right hand of the throne of God in Heaven. I ask You, Lord Jesus, to come into my life, forgive my sins, and make me Your child. I receive You now as my Saviour and Lord. I give my whole life to You. Teach me to follow You the rest of my days. I ask these things in Your Name. Thank You, Jesus. Amen."

Realize this: as you prayed, confessing with your mouth the faith in your heart (as in Romans 10:9-10), something took place within you — the little egg of faith united with the seed of the Word, and by the principle of divine life through the Holy Spirit a new life was conceived in your being. Jesus Christ is that "quickening Spirit" (I Corinthians 15:45), bringing you to new birth in Him. On the authority of His Word, according to John 1:12, you *are* a child of God; you are "born again". It doesn't depend upon how you feel — but upon what God has said.

I heard the story of a little boy who was sent home from school by his teacher to get his birth certificate. His mother, concerned about sending such an important document in the care of a small boy, pinned it to his coat and warned him not to dilly-dally on the way. But little boys find lots of interesting things to sidetrack them, and he was no different. It was a very forlorn child who returned from school that day to confess to his mother, "I lost my reason for being born."

I want you to know, now that you've been born again, that your birth certificate is safely registered in Heaven inscribed with the Word of God:

"To all who received Him, to those who believed in His Name, He gave the right to become children of God — children born not of natural descent... but born of God" (John 1:12-13 N.I.V.),

and also Galatians 3:26 which says:

"Ye are all the children of God by faith in Christ Jesus."

Some months ago while speaking at a women's luncheon, I told about the miracle of the new birth. Following the address, I asked if there was anyone who did not know for sure she was a child of God. I said that for even one person we would turn that meeting place into a "delivery room" to bring that one to birth, and I would help with her "labor pains". I led them in a prayer of confession and faith. I think we had quintuplets that day, and there was much rejoicing.

About two weeks later, I received a ten-page letter from one of these. I want to share parts of it with you:

"I just had to write to share all of this wonderful miracle that has happened to me. I had often read about being a child of God, and I tried to feel like one, but I just felt hollow and unworthy. I didn't feel loved. I felt very, very lonely."

She told me that she had been born to an unmarried teenage mother who had placed her for adoption. Her childhood was "a mess of lies and deceit." She believed she must be "a child of the devil" and said, "Until this day, my birthday, his dark evil spirit lurked in my mind feeding me cruel and miserable thoughts."

For ten years she had read every book she could find on philosophy, psychology and psychocybernetics, searching in vain for an understanding of herself and a sense of belonging. Then she concluded:

"When you talked about the new birth of the children of Jesus, I doubted I needed a rebirth even though I didn't feel like a child of God. I didn't feel like anybody's child. I knew my labor pains would last a million years, not just a few moments of prayer.

As you prayed, the labor pains you mentioned brought the tears, and I knew I needed to be reborn. Something happened to me. Jesus came into my heart right then. He opened His arms to me, wide and strong, and then I saw my name. Not just a little name, neat imprint, but written wide and high in wonderful letters. All I could say was: 'My name! My name!' It was written across Heaven, big and bold.

Jesus told me, 'You are not a Fatherless child. You have been born right into the family of God, your Father. You are His special, chosen child. How dearly you are wanted!'

The pain and terror of my lonely existence will no longer grip me. The peace of knowing who I am will be with me forever. I have just been born at age 31. I am still a baby in my loving Father's arms. I have a whole childhood of love ahead of me. Whoopee, whoopee! and Alleluia!"

Inherent in every human breast is a desire to worship and to touch something of the infinite. Driven by the intensity of this longing within, people search through drugs and the occult, through mysticism and religious rituals. Such was my friend, Tina. When she came to visit me, her face was etched with fear and her eyes seemed to be empty pools. She told me this sad story:

"I have been searching for so long through various philosophies and eastern religions to try to find some peace. Three years ago I went to a guru and received my mantra — I thought this would surely help.

Every day I have been sitting in my yoga stance meditating on my mantra, but something is happening to me: I feel as though I am floating out into nothingness, and I'm so afraid that one day I won't be able to find my way back. I'm presently going to a psychiatrist, but nothing helps."

I looked into her face and told her with gentle certainty: "There is hope. It is found in a Person. His Name is Jesus. That vacuum in your heart placed there by the Creator can only be satisfied by Him. Jesus Christ is not just the best answer; He is the only answer." Carefully I explained to her the Gospel of hope and salvation.

About a week later she returned and said, "I'm ready now. I want to accept Jesus. Please help me to pray. I've never prayed before, and I don't know how."

Together we voiced the prayer of confession and faith. She then sat quietly for a few moments, and I heard her whispering, "Thank You, Jesus." Then, as though suddenly remembering, she looked up and asked, "What about my mantra? How can I get rid of it? I was told I must never divulge it to any one."

"Tina," I said, "do you really want to be free?"

"I do! I do!" she cried.

"Then tell me the mantra, and in the Name of Jesus Christ the Son of God, you can be released from its power forever."

Without hesitation she spoke it, throwing it from her lips with finality. Then the prayer of faith in the all-powerful Name of Jesus loosed her from its bondage. Immediately a prayer of thanksgiving and praise broke from her heart in her own words. I saw the light come into her eyes. The fear slipped away like the dropping of a mask. She was free. Another remarkable thing about this story is that God wiped that word (her mantra) from *my* mind and memory too that very day. The ways of the Lord are great and marvellous in our eyes!

Tina was born again that day, "translated" from one kingdom (that of the power of darkness) into another, the kingdom of God's dear Son (Colossians 1:13). A whole new way of life lay before her. What now?

God doesn't abandon His children, nor leave them orphaned on somebody's doorstep. He Himself nourishes them through "the sincere milk of the Word" (I Peter 2:2). As from the mother life-giving and life-sustaining food flows into the infant at her breast, so the milk of the Word is "spirit and life" (John 6:63) to nourish and cause His little ones to grow and mature in Christ. As a mother's milk contains immunity bodies to protect the child from early infant diseases, so the "milk of the Word" protects against Satan's attacks and a hostile world. And there is no substitute.

Sometimes in the natural it is difficult for the new infant to suckle. The food is there but he must be helped to take it in. And this is also true in the spiritual. God didn't overlook a thing in His provision for His children. He has given us a family of brothers and sisters in Christ — a caring family to tend and strengthen the newborn babes in the faith. "We are members one of another" (Romans 12:5) — we need one another. For this reason I strongly encourage every new Christian to become a part of a local body of believers to learn to study and learn to grow.

Let me tell you some of the privileges which are yours as a child of God. Do you know that you are "an heir of God, and a joint-heir with Christ" (Rom. 8:17)? Because of our compassionate, understanding Jesus, the Son of God and our great High Priest Who is now seated in Heaven at the right hand of the majesty on high, you can come "boldly" (with confidence) into the very throne room of your Father to present your needs, to receive mercy and grace, and just to enjoy His wonderful Presence (Heb. 4:14-16).

I remember a toothpaste commercial we used to see on TV: a little boy came bursting into the room where his dad was presiding at a formal business meeting of austere gentlemen. He ran past them all calling wildly, "Daddy, Daddy! No cavities!" His dad arose from his chair at the head of that table, gathered the little fellow in his arms and said, "Son, that's the best news I've heard today!" Why did that child have such a privilege? Because he was a son *and* because he had utmost confidence in his father. There was a love relationship between them. That is how it is with us and our Heavenly Father when we know Jesus. Are you using your privileges?

Another thing He wants you to know is that you will *never* be alone nor forsaken. Oh, yes, you may be lonely for earthly companionship — but you can never be separated from the warmth of "His love which is shed abroad (or poured out) in your heart by the Holy Ghost which is given unto you" (Romans 5:5). Jesus promises that "He, the Comforter, would abide with you and in you forever" (John 14:16-17). That "Holy Spirit of promise" is His own "seal" upon you, guaranteeing to you that He is coming back to claim you, His "purchased possession" one day (Ephesians 1:13-14). He said, "I *will* come again, and receive you unto Myself; that where I am, there ye may be also" (John 14:3).

This is the glorious hope of the child of God. It is a terrible thing to be without hope, as was Sophie, who had been in a severe depression for three years. Some mornings she would phone me and say: "Joan, I can't get up today. It's too dark. I can't go on!"
For a number of weeks we worked together in counselling interviews. Then one day when I was at her home we seemed to reach an impasse. I

prayed in my heart, "Lord, show me where to go from here. I don't know the answers, but I know they are in Your Word. Please make me sensitive to Your Voice."

Immediately the Holy Spirit prompted me to read to her from the Scriptures about the second coming of Jesus Christ. I read I John 3:2.

"Beloved, now are we the sons of God, and it doth not yet appear what we shall be, but we know that when He shall appear, we shall be like Him, for we shall see Him as He is."

"I don't believe that," she said.

"You don't believe that?"

"No, I don't believe Jesus is coming back again," she said. "All my life I have been taught that the second coming of Jesus Christ occurred when I received Him into my heart as my Saviour. My brain won't accept that He is literally coming back again."

I read to her from the first chapter of Acts which describes the events when Jesus was taken up:

"This *same* Jesus which is taken up from you into Heaven, *shall* so come *in like manner* as you have seen Him go into Heaven" (Acts 1:11).

"My thinking won't accept it," she said. "My brain can't help it."

She needed a miracle. We have a big God, and He is the "greatest". Because I believe Him with all the intensity of my being, I asked Him to show me how to pray. I cupped my hands over her head, and I said, "By my faith I place on your head the helmet of salvation" which is part of the Christian's armor referred to in Ephesians 6:17. In I Thessalonians 5:8 it is called "the helmet of the *hope* of salvation." What is this hope? You will find it in I John 3:3. It is that Jesus is coming again to take us to be with Himself, and we are going to see Him."

I prayed that the Lord would make it real to her. I left her then, and on my way home I attended to some errands which took me about two hours. As I put the key into the lock of my door, I heard the phone ringing. I rushed in, lifted the receiver, and heard Sophie's excited voice.

"Joan, I don't know how to tell you. I can't explain it," she cried, "but I know that He is coming, and He is coming for me!"

Sophie's healing was beautiful — now she had something to live for. This is what it means to be a child of the King.

CHAPTER THREE

YOUR VITAL RESOURCE

"I wish to re-emphasize the meaning of "wholeness" because someone recently asked me: "If I am whole, does that mean I am perfect?" My answer was "No." Perhaps that will be a disappointment to some — and an intense relief to others. It all depends upon where we stand. If we demand perfection of ourselves, we will hit the bottom when we fail; if we demand it of others, we will become judgmental and critical.

The husband of a friend of mine became a Christian. She thought that right now (stat) all their marital problems would be solved and he would turn into an instant angel. Wouldn't that be beautiful? But it doesn't happen that way. We have to grow and it takes time. The trouble is we are an instant generation. Our shelves are full of instant products to satisfy the instant appetites of our families as they rush in and out of the house in between their chock-full schedules. We do not become spiritual giants over night.

It would seem that when we think of "perfection" we associate it with "flawlessness" — such as a perfect diamond. When the Bible uses the word "perfect", the meaning in most instances from the Hebrew and Greek is "complete" or "whole" or "to fit thoroughly". It is perfection in relation to completeness. In Matthew 5:48 Jesus said:

"Be ye therefore perfect, even as your Father which is in heaven is perfect."

Because of the "therefore" we must look back to the context where we find Him speaking of right relationships in every area of our beings.

The heart must be "pure" before God; the emotions must be ruled by love and mercy, not anger and hate; the mind must dwell on the true purpose of His coming which was to fulfil not to destroy; the body must be disciplined even to "plucking out" the eye that offends in lust and adultery; and our relationship with others must be that of the "peacemaker". As each dimension of our lives is guided by our love to God and brought under the control of His righteous principles, there is a "fitting together" which brings a harmonious unity or "wholeness".

But, my friend, God has not finished with us yet — one day we *are* going to be "flawless". Hear these words from the pen of Jude:

"Unto Him Who is able to keep you from falling, and to present you faultless (without blemish, blame, or spot) before the presence of His glory with exceeding joy.."

and it is no wonder Jude concludes such a fantastic pronouncement with this glorious doxology:

"To the only wise God, Our Saviour, be glory and majesty, dominion and power, both now and ever. Amen" (Jude 24-25).

In the meantime He is preparing us for that day: "We are His workmanship" (Eph. 2:10); He is "conforming us to the image of His Son" (Rom. 8:29), and He will finish the job (Phil. 1:6). God does not make failures — He makes winners. Hallelujah!

But maybe it's the "in the meantime" you are worried about. Perhaps you are saying, "The standards of the Sermon on the Mount are too high for me to attain. I could never love God with all my being as He commands. It's too much for me."

You're right — it's too much for any of us. God knows that too, and He has made available to us an abundantly sufficient resource. When we were born again, we not only became His children with all the privileges we have already mentioned, but our communion with Him was restored, making it possible for us to tap the very fountain of Life in Christ. Hear this:

"If, when we were enemies, we were reconciled to God by the death of His Son, *much more,* being reconciled, we shall be saved (sōzō — kept safe and sound) by His life" (Rom. 5:10).

The reconciliation was just the beginning — the "much more" is the superlative power of His resurrection Life operative within our beings day after day, bringing wholeness and healing. Jesus spoke of this power as "rivers of living water":

"He that believeth on Me, as the Scripture hath said, out of his belly (inner being) shall flow rivers of living water. (But this spake He of the Spirit, which they that believe on Him should receive: for the Holy Ghost was not yet given; because Jesus was not yet glorified") (John 7:38-39).

Jesus Christ has now been glorified — the Holy Spirit has been given. Peter stood up on the day of Pentecost and proclaimed:

"This Jesus hath God raised up, whereof we are witnesses. Therefore being by the right hand of God exalted, and having received of the Father the promise of the Holy Spirit, He hath shed forth this which ye now see and hear" (Acts 2:32-33).

The Holy Spirit is here — He has never been recalled. To the believer He is the flowing river of the resurrection Life of Christ. This power released within us by the Spirit is the *same power* which raised Jesus from the dead.

Oh, that we might really grasp the magnificence of this in our daily lives! Here it is:

"If the Spirit of Him that raised up Jesus from the dead dwell in you, He that raised up Christ from the dead shall also *quicken* your *mortal* bodies by His Spirit that dwelleth in you" (Rom. 8:11).

Not only will we be quickened in the ultimate resurrection which will be the total fulfilment, but we have a foretaste now in the "quickening" of these mortal bodies — these bodies that we live in that hurt and suffer pain and depression. My prayer for you who read this book is that of Paul expressed in Ephesians 1:18-20 — that you may *know* and *understand:*

"...what is the *exceeding greatness* of His power *to us* (and *in us*) who believe, *according* to the working of His mighty power, which He wrought in Christ when he raised Him from the dead, and set Him at His own right hand in the heavenly places...."

This is the power which sets us "free from the law of sin and death" (Romans 8:2) which has bound and shackled us to the old carnal nature of our natural birth.

I want you to understand that you do not have to hobble along barely making it. There is a glorious victorious life for you. Why not come out of the shadows and start living? By the help of the Holy Spirit I will try to make it as simple, clear and practical as I can on paper. I will refer you to the diagram again to show you how to reach out in faith that the river of His Life may flow bountifully into your being.

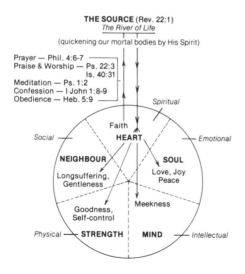

You will notice that the communication lines from the area of the spirit, the devotional part of our beings, are two-way. Everything we receive from God comes through the avenue of faith. "Without faith it is impossible to please Him." He only asks us to "believe that He is, and that He is a rewarder of them that diligently seek Him" (Hebrews 11:6). He has not asked us to place our faith in some fantasy or mystical unreality, but on the solid absolutes of His Word which are unchangeable and settled forever in Heaven. His Word can bear the weight of all our trust.

It is essential for us to know how to keep these communication lines open that we might receive a continuous flow of the Life-giving stream. The irreversible injunction of Scripture is: "Draw nigh to God, and He will draw nigh to you" (James 4:8). Our part is clearly defined and consists of five outlets of our communion with God by faith: 1) *Prayer* — Phil. 4:6-7; 2) *Praise and worship* — Isa. 40:31, Psalm 22:3; 3) *Meditation* — Ps. 1:2; 4) *Confession* — I John 1:8-9; 5) *Obedience* — Hebrews 5:9.

We must be careful to give each one of these its place in our daily lives and that we do not over-emphasize one at the expense of another. Each is significant and vital; each is a powerful force.

Satan seeks to vitiate every expression of man toward God. One area of his attack we see today is meditation. T.M. (or transcendental meditation) is Satan's counterfeit of a Biblical principle. By the use of incantations and mantras the followers of T.M. reach out into the occult. Often they are unaware that the vacuum created in their minds is infiltrated by demonic powers — until it is too late.

"Meditation" for the child of God is positive. It is not the meaningless repetition of verses of Scripture, nor of the Name of Jesus, as though these were magical words. We do not worship an "unknown God" Who is far off and unreachable. We *were once* far away from Him but we *are now* brought near by the Blood of Christ (Eph. 2:13), and we know Him in truth and reality. Meditation for the Christian is not a mystical ritual; it is not blanking out the mind.

"But his delight is in the law of the Lord; and in His law doth he meditate day and night" (Psalm 1:2).

To meditate means to *reflect upon*, to *study*, and to *ponder*. Our devotional time each day should include a quiet waiting before the Lord, reading His Word and asking the Holy Spirit to speak to our hearts.

We must not let our lives subsist only on meetings, as wonderful and exciting as they may be. It is in the "secret place" of quiet reflection and communion that we come to know Him personally on that one-to-One basis. During my years of counselling I have found so often that those who return despondent and defeated have neglected this vital resource.

Such was Ellen, who didn't think she had time in her working day for devotions. Soon she was suffering from spiritual malnutrition — her old habits surfaced to torment her. "Ellen, it would be better to take ten minutes in communion with Jesus each day than none at all," I said.

"Discipline your thoughts to focus on Him — make every minute significant. Then write a verse from your Scripture portion on a piece of paper, slip it in your pocket and 'snack on it' during the day until it actually becomes a part of your 'think'."

She decided to try it. Her devotional time became more and more meaningful and joyful to her with each passing day. Those daily verses became a source of strength, and her Christian life took on a new vibrancy.

We have the sure promises of Jesus that:

"...the Comforter, which is the Holy Ghost, Whom the Father will send in My Name, He shall teach you all things, and bring all things to your remembrance, whatsoever I have said unto you" (John 14:26).

But He can bring to our remembrance only that which we have stored away in our cranial computers — our minds. Sometimes we are like stubborn children: we don't feel like chewing, swallowing and digesting the Word. So we just hold it in our minds for a few moments and then spit it out. Therefore it does not get down to our inward parts to nourish us. Other times we stuff ourselves with chapter after chapter until we get spiritual indigestion from eating too much too quickly. The next day we say, "I don't feel like reading today; I read so much yesterday and it didn't do me much good — in fact, I felt dull and heavy afterwards." These are the things I encounter when counselling people who are not growing in their Christian lives.

It is a *steady, balanced* diet we need, allowing the Holy Spirit to ingrain it into the very fabric of our beings, that it might become "life and health to all our flesh" — a principle clearly defined in Proverbs 4:2-22. There are no shortcuts — and no substitutes. But the dividends are incalculable for the one who learns the secret of true Biblical meditation.

"He shall be like a tree planted by the rivers of water, that bringeth forth his fruit in his season; his leaf also shall not wither; and whatsoever he doeth shall prosper" (Psalm 1:3).

Remember that the communication lines of the spiritual life are two-way. As we keep the channel open by faith, through the principles I have outlined for you, the Life of Jesus Christ flows in and through our beings, producing fruit in every area — as shown on the chart.

For many years I struggled so hard to bear fruit — love, joy, peace, longsuffering, gentleness, goodness, faith, meekness, temperance (self-control). I didn't seem to have any of these in my life. One day when I was discouraged and depressed, I sat on the grass under the trees. Looking up to Heaven, I said, "Lord, where is the beautiful fruit which should abound in the life of the Christian? No matter how hard I try, I produce nothing but leaves. I'm empty and barren." I was gazing up at my apple tree laden with fruit, and I thought, "That tree doesn't seem to struggle to bear apples. Of course not! It bears apples because it is an apple tree." And Jesus whispered to my heart:

> "Remain in Me, and I will remain in you. No branch can bear fruit by itself; it must remain in the vine. Neither can you bear fruit unless you remain in Me.
> I am the vine; you are the branches. If a man remains in Me and I in Him, *he will bear much fruit;* apart from Me you can do nothing" (John 15:4-5 N.I.V.).

He taught me the secret of the "abiding" life that day. I had discovered that all the trying in the world can never make us like Jesus, but His indwelling life through the Word makes us "naturally" *partakers* or sharers *of the divine nature.* (II Pet. 1:4).

CHAPTER FOUR

ROADBLOCKS ON THE WAY TO WHOLENESS

Now that we have learned how the spiritual dimension of our lives is quickened and how it relates to every area of our being as a channel of the resurrection life of Jesus Christ, we can realize the significance of Proverbs 4:23 which states:

"Keep thine heart with all diligence; for out of it are the issues of life,"

and "A sound heart is the life of the flesh" (Prov. 14:30).

In view of these great truths, why is it that so many Christians do not experience this life-giving flow of the Spirit in their daily lives? For some, life is drudgery, depression and defeat. If you meet them on the street, you are almost afraid to ask them, "How are you today?" lest you start them on their tale of woe. For others who seem to be so happy on the surface, there is a constant battle with psychosomatic illness. The doctor doesn't know what to do other than treat the symptoms to make life a little more bearable — so the arthritic continues with his aspirin, the coronary keeps going with nitroglycerin, and the ulcer victims treat themselves with antacids.

Somehow the River is hindered on its course — it is not bearing life and healing throughout the whole being. Has the River been depleted? Has it lost its power? Has God been fickle and shut it off? No! No! With Him is "no variableness, neither shadow of turning" (James 1:17). We are the ones who throw up the roadblocks and who dam up the River. Somehow we have neglected the spiritual and the issues of life have ceased to flow. We may have isolated our devotional life knowingly, because we do not want it to interfere with any other facet of our lives. Or we may be doing it unwittingly.

I will show you three ways this can happen: 1) By living in formalism and ritualism. 2) By living on past experiences. 3) By living in unconfessed sin.

1) *By living in formalism and ritualsim.* We may attend our church faithfully, tithe regularly, teach Sunday School, sing in the choir or serve in areas of ministry. We may say a prayer each day and read some Bible verses. Then, having fulfilled our obligation, we tuck our devotional duties back in their little box, close the lid, and go out to live as we please. We are

in effect saying, "God, I have paid my respects to you. Now stay out of the rest of my life, I want to run it my way."

In II Timothy 3:5 Paul speaks of those who "have a form of godliness, but deny the power thereof" to transform their lives. If we do this, we suffer terrible internal consequences because we have, of our own volition, shut out the Life of Christ. The subsequent guilt, fear, and anger will cause drastic repercussions within.

2) *By living on past experiences.* Some of us allow our lives to revolve around some spiritual experience of the past. We live in retrospection. We settle down on that wonderful experience. We are like Peter who wanted to build three tabernacles on the Mount of Transfiguration. It may have been authentic, legitimate, glorious and wonderful, but if we pin our faith on that experience alone, we are on very shaky ground. What will we do when the thrill has waned and clouds of doubt attack us? Will we cry out, "Jesus, where are You? I can't feel You today — have You deserted me?"

Dr. Francis Schaeffer has said: "faith is not a blind leap in the dark." It is based on eternal absolutes — the Word of God. I *know* Jesus has not deserted because His Word says :

> "I will never leave thee, nor forsake thee" (Hebrews 13:5). "Lo, I am with you always" (Matt. 28:20).

It is upon these truths I stand.

Peter records his experience on the Mount:

> "We ... were eyewitnesses of His majesty ... there came ... a voice to Him from the excellent glory, This is My beloved Son, in whom I am well pleased" (II Peter 1:16-17).

What a magnificent, glorious happening! But then Peter continues:

> "We have *also a more sure word* of prophecy; whereunto ye do well that ye *take heed,* as unto a light that shineth in a dark place, until the day dawn, and the day star arise in your hearts" (II Peter 1:19).

What is this "more sure word of prophecy"? It is the Holy Scriptures. Faith, without the knowledge of the Word, would indeed be "a blind leap in the dark." Faith cannot be divorced from God's Word because it is produced and sustained by it (see Romans 10:17).

3) *By living in unconfessed sin.* By living in unconfessed sin and impenitence we pull down the blinds and shut out the light. You see, Jesus Christ is life, and that life is the light of men, as shown in John 1:4. If we shut out the river of life, we also cut off the light — and darkness creeps in upon us. Isaiah 59:1-2 records these words:

> "The Lord's hand is not shortened, that it cannot save; neither His ear heavy, that it cannot hear:"

(His power has not changed nor diminished one iota.)

"But your iniquities have separated between you and your God, and your sins have hid His face from you, that He will not hear."

(You were the one who shut Him out.) The Psalmist says,
"If I *regard* iniquity in my heart, the Lord will not hear me" (Psalm 66:18).

The Hebrew word here which is translated "regard" literally means "see". If I see sin in my heart and do nothing about it, I shut myself off from Him. But we do not have to remain in the darkness. God has made a gracious provision for us when we turn to Him in true repentance. He promises us that:

"If we confess our sins, He is faithful and just to forgive us our sins, and to cleanse us from all unrighteousness" (I John 1:9).

Let us also take comfort in the words of I John 2:1:

"My dear children, I write this to you so that you will not sin."

In other words, "I don't want you to sin." But He knows all our weaknesses and how often we fail. Therefore He has provided hope for us:

"If anybody does sin, we have One Who speaks to the Father in our defense — Jesus Christ, the righteous One" (I John 2:1 N.I.V.).

We are human and therefore we are not perfect. It is such a comfort to know that when we do stumble or fall or grieve Him when our faith is small, we can come to Him and be forgiven immediately. On one occasion I was troubled for many days because of something I had done. Although I had made it right as far as I could, it still seemed to cloud my prayer time, and each day I wasted part of this precious time with Him begging for forgiveness. Finally, when I stopped pleading long enough to listen, I heard Him say into my heart: "How long are you going to ask Me to forgive you? Don't you believe My Word? I have forgiven you at the Cross."

"Oh, yes, I do believe," I said, "and I accept it now." Then His peace descended upon me, and I was able to enter into praise, worship, and intercession without that black cloud hanging over me any longer. What a release it was!

Let me show you now how our whole person is affected when we are cut off from the Light of Life in Christ — and the controlling influence of the Holy Spirit 1) in the emotions, 2) in the mind, 3) in the body and 4) in our social relationship.

1) *In the emotions.* Negative emotions tend to predominate, and we find ourselves putting more and more significance upon feelings. We become

what I call "yo-yo Christians" — tossed between the highs and lows of our emotional instability. Without the counter balance of the positive (love, joy, peace, security and confidence), we are overcome by our hatreds, fears, bitternesses and insecurities which seep like sludge into every area of our beings. The Bible shows us the inevitable results:

"A calm and undisturbed mind and heart are the life and health of the body, but *envy, jealousy,* and *wrath* are as rottenness of the bones" (Proverbs 14:30 Amplified).

Furthermore, in the desperate search for a counter balance, many become involved in delusive cults and practices. Such was my friend Kirsten who told me she had been searching for peace all her life. Her shelves were lined with books on philosophies, mysticism and various religions — all of which she studied deeply in her desperate need.

One day she asked me: "Do you think Jesus could help?"

"You've tried everything else," I said. "Why don't you put Him to the test?" We knelt in my little kitchen. Humbly and honestly she asked Jesus Christ to come into her life as her Saviour and satisfy the yearning of her heart. The next morning she came bouncing into the house and excitedly reported what had happened.

"This is the first time I can remember waking up to find peace in my heart," she said. "At last I have found Him." Then she added, "I'm going to get rid of all those books — I won't need them any more." Soon she won her husband and children to the Lord, and Jesus became the Prince of Peace to that home.

Sometimes we may try to live in a make-believe world of joy. As a teenager, I lived for fun and laughter. When I was out with my friends I could put on a good act — willing to do anything for kicks. But my counterfeit world was a fantasy. When I lay in my bed alone at night the whole thing would burst like a bubble leaving me disillusioned, and the pillow would be wet with my tears. It wasn't until I met Jesus Christ that I found a joy that was real.

If our emotions become the ruling factor in our lives, we may seek for a continuous high. Striving for this, many go down the dead-end streets of drugs, illicit sex or any type of gratification through sensory pleasures.

Gary was brought up in a Christian home, but he thought there must be an easier way to get "high" than becoming a Christian. His friends told him what a great feeling would come from smoking marijuana. He decided to give it a try. "This is really great!" he thought. "Wow!" All his problems drifted away as he floated on his "high". But somehow he couldn't maintain it, and he had to keep taking more to get up there. Soon stronger drugs were necessary, and he would think, "At last I've made it. I'm up there now."

But always there would be that terrible drop into melancholy when the drug wore off until — he told me — he knew he was in a whirlpool that was going faster and faster, sucking him into a black abyss. He was scared. He knew that he was almost at the point of no return. Then out of his desperation he cried, "Lord, save me!"

As he described the change Jesus had made in his life, he said to me, "Now I know that no one can be 'high' all the time. I have found in Jesus a joy that is stable. It never lifts me away up and then drops me further down. It is a settled peace. It is secure, and I know that when I wake up in the morning it will still be with me."

Ruth also lived on emotions — it was the fantasy world of TV soap operas. She told me she hardly knew what was real or unreal any more. She didn't even know her own identity. She took upon herself the personality of each actor until she became a person of many faces, and she didn't know which was really herself. In her confusion and helplessness she wept before the Lord and made a total commitment of her life to Him — including her emotional being. With His help she was able to find her real self and the bondage of the TV was broken.

Remember that emotions are an intrinsic part of each one of us, and when we give them to Jesus He opens for us a wonderful capacity for His joy. It is "His joy" because He said:

"These things have I spoken unto you, that *My joy* might remain in you, and that your joy might be *full*" (John 15:11).

This is not a surface rapture which ebbs and flows like the tide. It is not an effervescent thing which fizzles out like an Alka Seltzer. Because it is His gift — His joy, it *remains* settled, stable, a deep "well of salvation" within us (Isaiah 12:3). Yes, we will weep — Jesus wept at the graveside of Lazarus. We will be sorrowful, yet in the midst of it there will be a rejoicing (II Cor. 6:10). Is this a paradox? No. Because, you see, the joy of the Christian is not dependent upon outward circumstances but upon an absolute. Jesus said:

"Rejoice because your names are written in Heaven" (Luke 10:20).

Nothing on this earth can "separate us from the love of God which is in Christ Jesus our Lord..."

"...neither death, nor life, nor angels, nor principalities, nor powers, nor things present, nor things to come, nor height, nor depth, nor any creature..." (Romans 8:38-39).

Nothing! Paul even says in the preceding verse:

"In all these things we are more than conquerors through him that loved us."

Did you ever see a defeated conqueror? Though still *in* the midst of the battle, we rejoice because of His victory which *is* already accomplished.

What do you do about those mornings when everything, including your spirit, seems drab and joyless? You would love to crawl back in bed and bury your head, but you know that somehow you have to face the duties of the day. Let me share a secret with you. One of my childhood memories is of a well in our back yard which provided our water. Sometimes the pump would creak and groan, but as we kept working it, the water would finally gush out in abundance.

I have found that when I feel dry and down, if I prime the pump of praise, regardless of how creaky it may be, it will bring up the springs of joy from the well deep within me — the same well spoken of by Isaiah. God does inhabit the praises of His people, as shown in Psalm 22:3. I know this is a Biblical principle. Therefore, although I may not *feel like* praising Him, I offer Him a "sacrifice of praise...the fruit of my lips" (Hebrews 13:15). I *speak* the words of thanksgiving and adoration, not because of how *I feel* but because of *Who He is.* Then from out of my inmost being the river starts to flow again in a crystal stream of life and joy.

Is your pump rusty from neglect? And have you wondered why you are so dry? Why don't you try praising?

2) *In the mind.* What happens when the intellect is cut off from the source of spiritual life? It is barren and without spiritual perception. How clearly this is recorded in I Cor. 2:14 in the N.I.V.

"The man without the Spirit does not accept the things that come from the Spirit of God, for they are foolishness to him, and he *cannot understand* them, because they are spiritually discerned."

One day someone said scoffingly to me: "I have read your Bible from cover to cover — it never did me any good." Why? Because reading God's Word without an honest and sincere heart profits nothing. The reading itself is non-productive and lifeless. It is just as Paul has stated:

"The Word...did not profit them, not being mixed with faith in them that heard it" (Hebrews 4:2).

I may stuff my mind with knowledge, but without the enlightenment of the Holy Spirit, I become a kind of encyclopedia of computerized facts — an arid desert. God longs for us to truly know Him. Therefore, He speaks through Hosea as much today as when He inspired Hosea to write:

"...I desired mercy, and not sacrifice; and the knowledge of God more than burnt offerings" (Hosea 6:6).

He sent His Son "made in the likeness of men" (Phil. 2:7) that He might reveal to us His great heart of love and forgiveness. He gave us His Word that we might "*know* that we have eternal life" and "*believe* on the Name of the Son of God" (I John 5:13). "Life eternal" is to "*know* the only true God, and Jesus Christ, Whom He has sent" (John 17:3). He sent the Holy

Spirit to abide with us forever — the eternal Witness within (Romans 8:16).

"I will put my laws into their hearts, and in their *minds* will I write them" (Heb. 10:16).

He says this so that heart and mind might be fully integrated in wholeness and health. He has made provision for us to touch Him in reality.

If we neglect His Word, our minds become a vacuum for the barrage of negative thought imposed upon us by the world in which we live. Headlines from the magazine racks strategically placed near the check-out stands in supermarkets, subtle innuendos portrayed on the TV screen or picked up from the incessant chattering of the radio — all imprint themselves on the mind even though we are not consciously absorbing them. Our only defense is to fill our minds with the Word of God. In doing this, we do not allow a vacuum to form.

We may read the Bible religiously, but if we do not obey its precepts nor appropriate its promises for ourselves, it becomes non-productive in our lives. If we hear and obey, we shall be like the man who built on the rock and was unmoved by the storm — as Jesus recorded in Luke 6:47-49. But if we hear and do not obey His Word, our house will fall when the storms beat against it.

According to Proverbs 23:7 we really are what we think, so we must guard very carefully what we process into our minds. The mind under the control of the Holy Spirit does not feed on garbage whether it is sensuality and lust, godless philosophies, horoscopes or cultism, which plunge the whole person into despair and darkness.

Jim was a teenager who had saturated his mind with pornography. He bowed at the Cross one night, and all the accumulated filth spewed out of him in great racking sobs. Finally he said, "Mrs. James, you have no idea how evil the books and magazines are that I have been reading. I was completely bound by them, but now Jesus has cleaned me up and I am free. I am going home to burn all that trash." The next night he said, "I have been burning stuff all day and there is still more, but I won't stop until every trace is gone."

May God help us to program these minds to a Bible "think", and may our hearts respond so that we will neither think nor act lust, evil, failure, unbelief, depression — or the myriad things that serve to rob and destroy.

3) *In the physical body.* Does the spiritual life really relate to the physical body? Oh, yes, indeed it does. We cannot control the appetites of the flesh without the inflow of spiritual life. Left to our own whims and natural desires, we fail miserably. Like the story I once heard about a woman standing by a roadside market, when she noticed a driverless car slowly coming down an incline. Seemingly it was headed straight for the fruit stand. In a moment of decision she rushed to the car, pulled open the door, jumped in and stomped on the brake. As she sat gasping at her audacity, the red face of a man appeared at the window.

"Did you see what I did?" she cried. "Wasn't that wonderful?"

"Yes, it certainly was," he replied rather sardonically. "I was pushing."

That may be a comical story, but it aptly illustrates how well we bungle things when we insist on being in the driver's seat.

Today we live in such a permissive society that people often think because everyone is doing it, it must be okay. But a psychiatrist once asked, "If there is no such thing as sin, why is there so much guilt?" Although our actions may be socially acceptable, we still bear the inevitable consequences within ourselves.

A number of Christian couples who have come for pre-marital counselling have confessed great guilt and unhappiness because they had allowed themselves to become involved in a sexual relationship. One couple was convicted and troubled — and lashing out at one another, each blamed the other. It was to be a number of months before they could be married, and they both said, "What will we do? We can't go on like this."

"If you are willing to follow the rules," I said, "I can help you." I told them that God did not set parameters for living in order to make life unpleasant for us, but rather to protect us from sorrow and hurt. They had stepped over the lines God had laid down, and they must come to Him for forgiveness. Then I asked them if they were willing to make a decisive commitment of their bodies to Jesus Christ from that day until their wedding day when they would come together in the blessing of the Lord. They bowed before the Lord and made this commitment together.

I warned them that it would not be easy unless they disciplined their dating and their living, and I gave them some stern rules to guide them. They kept their promise to one another and to God. They brought that area of their lives under the control of the Holy Spirit. Soon I noticed a new respect and admiration in their eyes for one another. They were married about a year later, and after some months had passed I receive a phone call: "Mrs. James, we are so glad we made that dedication to God, and that He helped us to keep it. Our marriage is just what we had always dreamed it would be."

Because we are so aware of the physical, we tend to lay great emphasis upon the body, as though it were of utmost significance. We will pamper it, indulge it, and give in to its every whim, or we will swing the pendulum to the other extreme and beat and drive our bodies beyond endurance until they break under the stress. There is the "workoholic" who cannot stop to rest. There is the faddist who deprives his body of necessary foods while over-emphasizing others. And then there are those of us who minister who are overcome by the multitude of needs which face us every day and in our longing to help, we drive ourselves into the ground.

I know — it happens to me. Then I have to go before the Lord and examine my motives. I reassess my values, weigh the priorities and learn to flow with God instead of running around on my own steam. There is a place of balance, and it is found under the control of the Holy Spirit. God has given me this body. I must keep it in peak condition for Him, lest by my own foolishness I cut down my efficiency before my time.

May I remind you that "wholeness" is not "perfection" but rather, every area of my being brought into harmony through the inflowing of the resurrection Life of Jesus Christ.

These physical bodies of ours are far from perfect. They are only our temporary dwellings. The final redemption of our bodies spoken of in Romans 8:23 will take place when we see Jesus, and

> "...this corruptible" puts on "incorruption, and this mortal" puts on "immortality, *then* shall be brought to pass the saying that is written, Death is swallowed up in victory" (I Corinthians 15:54).

I met a man some time ago whose name was Richard Miller. This man was born without arms or legs. All he had was a stump of a body and a head, and yet he was a "whole person" radiating the life of Jesus Christ as he travelled about in a ministry of evangelism.

I have known several Mongoloid people whose love and devotion have enriched my life. One of these, a dear little man, came up to me one day. Grasping my hand in his warm one, he said earnestly, "Mrs. James, I pray for you every day." Even writing this brings the tears to my eyes. Was he less than a whole person? No, because he had given all that he had to Jesus. There was a harmony in his life which comes only from commitment, and it does not depend upon our I.Q.

As we bring our bodies into submission to Christ, as Paul stated in I Corinthians 9:27, and we are "crucified with Christ" (Gal. 2:20) no longer catering to its fleshly appetites, then the life which we "now live in the flesh" will be that of resurrection life — new, radiant, vibrant (as expressed in Romans 6:4).

One young couple told me: "We had thoroughly messed up our lives and our marriage. Then we decided we had been in the driver's seat long enough. We moved over and gave the keys to Jesus. Since that day things have begun to fall into place in a new harmony. Now we don't make any decisions without asking His direction first."

4) *In our social relationships.* Without the inflow of spiritual life, our social relationships become self-centred and manipulative. If our whole lives revolve around the "I", this is what can happen:

a) With total unconcern for others we will step on, push around, or manipulate anyone who is in the way of our own ego.

I have seen this "dog-eat-dog" attitude destroy every cooperative effort among a concerned team of working people. It eats away at the very roots.

b) Always wishing to pad our ego we will lay aside our own personal convictions in order to be men pleasers. We will become vacillating and unstable, tossed about by the opinions of others.

c) Or living in a little world all of our own, we will withdraw ourselves from society.

How different it is when the social area of our lives is under the control of the Holy Spirit. The Bible says:

"When a man's ways please the Lord, He maketh even His enemies to be at peace with him" (Proverbs 16:7).

This does not mean "peace at any cost" — even to the abrogation of our convictions. God has shown us the way to relate to others in His Word:

"But the wisdom that comes from heaven is first of all pure; then peace-loving, considerate, submissive, full of mercy and good fruit, impartial and sincere. Peacemakers who sow in peace raise a harvest of righteousness" (James 3:17-18 N.I.V.).

It is a simple formula made possible by the daily inflow of the River of life into every area of our beings.

Yes, there are roadblocks on the way to "wholeness," but they are of our own making. Perhaps you, my reader, may wish to make that decisive commitment of every area of your being to Him right now. Do as the young couple did — get out of the driver's seat and give the keys to Jesus. Will you stop at this moment to make this your prayer:

"Lord Jesus, I have been running my own life too long, and it hasn't turned out well. I need You. I don't know how to choose my way. I give my whole life to You, and I ask You to direct all my paths. Teach me to walk with You in total commitment from this day. Amen."

CHAPTER FIVE

WHAT HAPPENED TO THIS BODY?

There are many causes of sickness, and I would like to relate a few of these for your consideration: 1) Those brought about by our own foolishness or disobedience. 2) Those which come as a result of living in a sin-cursed and polluted world. 3) Those which come as the result of accidents. 4) Those which are psychogenic.

1) *Those brought about by our own foolishness or disobedience.* Many times we do not obey the simple principles of healthful living which are laid down in the Word of God. Often we ignore the promptings of our own common sense, and then when our bodies break down under the strain we cry out to God: "Why did You let this happen to me?"

2) *Those which come as a result of living in a sin-cursed and polluted world.* These sicknesses would include genetic disorders with which we are born or which pre-dispose us to certain diseases. God does not put us in a glass showcase. He is not raising hothouse plants, but "trees of righteousness, the planting of the Lord, that He might be glorified" (Isaiah 61:3).

3) *Those which come as the result of accidents.* I think of someone like Joni who became a quadraplegic as the result of a diving accident and whose story is in print. I think of my own nephew who suffered brain damage from an injury, or of others who have been disfigured by fire. These are only a few — the list is multitudinous.

I believe in miracles. I have seen those who were raised from death beds and those whose crippled, deformed bodies God has completely restored. But I have also seen those who have died triumphantly in the faith, and others who have lived victoriously in their tortured bodies. What is the answer? Do we beat and condemn ourselves because we do not seem to be able to attain the faith which would release the Hand of God on their behalf? If this were so, we would live in continual defeat and condemnation. But the Bible says:

"There is therefore *now* no condemnation to them which are in Christ Jesus" (Rom. 8:1).

There is a place of peace for the child of God — it is in the fact that God is sovereign and that:

"He performeth the thing that is appointed for me" (Job 23:14), and

"He knoweth the way that I take: when He hath tried me, I *shall* come forth as gold" (Job 23:10).

I remind you that these physical bodies are our *temporary* dwellings. The final redemption of our bodies spoken of in Romans 8:23 will be when

".... this corruptible puts on incorruption, and this mortal puts on immortality, and then shall be brought to pass the saying that is written, Death is swallowed up in victory" (I Cor. 15:54).

Death is an enemy, but take heart for "the last enemy to be destroyed is death" (I Cor. 15:26).

In the meantime, even we who have received "the firstfruits of the Spirit, groan within ourselves waiting... for the redemption of our bodies" (Rom. 8:23). Yet in the "waiting" period, the "Rivers of Living Water" flow continuously into and out of our inmost beings. Because these finite earthen bodies could not contain it all (or we would immediately be translated into Heaven — and He hasn't finished with us down here yet), He gives us "the firstfruits of the Spirit" or a foretaste, which is our security or pledge —

"Which is the earnest of our inheritance until the redemption of the purchased possession" (Ephesians 1:14).

Let us look up. Let us rejoice. Our future is *assured.* It is guaranteed!

"Our citizenship is in heaven. And we eagerly await a Saviour from there, the Lord Jesus Christ, who, by the power that enables Him to bring everything under His control, *will transform our lowly bodies* so they will *be like His glorious body*" (Phil. 3:20-21 N.I.V.).

Therefore we can identify with Paul who said:

"I eagerly expect and hope that I will in no way be ashamed, but will have sufficient courage so that *now* as always Christ will be exalted in my body, *whether by life or by death.* For to me to live is Christ and to die is gain" (Phil. 1:20-21 N.I.V.).

What a way to live! And what a way to die! I have been at many death beds, and I can say Christians die well. Recently we laid my youngest sister to rest, who had fought valiantly with a malignant brain tumor through two surgeries. As it finally tapped her life, she fell peacefully asleep in Jesus. I was in the midst of a seminar during this time.

My heart was aching — for we are human. As I spoke on this particular evening, I found myself expressing in words what was truly in my heart:

"The death of a Christian is not a victory for Satan but a triumph for Heaven. Now that loved one is out of the reach of Satan's attacks for ever."

As I said this, my spirit was lifted in an expressible rejoicing, and I could say as Paul did, "As sorrowful, yet always rejoicing" (II Cor. 6:10). Now at last I understood what had often seemed to me to be a paradox.

4) *Those which are psychogenic.* There is still another cause of illness which has risen to major proportions in our stress-laden society. It is that which is psychogenic — the origin is not physical, but rooted in the psyche. The symptoms are manifested in the body or "soma", and it is called "psychosomatic illness."

These conditions account for a very high percentage of patients being treated by doctors today. I have heard that seventy-five percent of prescriptions written by doctors are for nervous conditions such as angina, ulcers, migraine headaches, colitis — to name just a few. In order to understand this, we must have some knowledge of the operation of the subconscious mind.

We must realize that our adult responses and reactions are largely the result of the pre-programming of our childhood. A newspaper article printed May 17, 1977 quotes the findings published by the National Geographic Magazine that the brain apparently functions as a super-computer. Every experience that has ever happened in our lives has been indelibly imprinted upon our subconscious minds. This has been proven and demonstrated in medical science.

The pioneer in this field of research was a neuro-surgeon from McGill University in Montreal, Dr. Wilder Penfield — who died in June, 1976. In the report of his death in the *Vancouver Sun* it was noted:

"Perhaps the most dramatic of Dr. Penfield's discoveries was that the brain could be stimulated electrically to 'play back' events recorded by the brain but not implanted in normal memory."

These experiments were conducted during the course of brain surgery when the patient on the operating table was under a local anesthetic, and hence fully conscious. Through a window in the skull, Dr. Penfield inserted a galvanized probe which carried a weak electrical current, and touched a portion of the cerebral cortex of the brain.

Immediately, as though portrayed on a three-dimensional screen in front of him, the patient saw events of his childhood that had been completely blocked out from his conscious mind. He saw himself. He heard certain music associated with his childhood. He saw events, some traumatic and some happy. He was able to describe them in detail. They were not jumbled. They were precise. He saw them, and not only could he describe them but he could describe the emotions which he felt as they occurred many years ago.

The conclusions reached by the doctors were that familiar experiences could be projected into a person's consciousness whether he wanted to remember or not. A song, a place, a time, a situation could progress and unfold like a familiar play, with the patient being both actor and audience. The brain acts like a tape recorder with the added dimension of the feelings which are recorded and locked into the experiences, and they are available for replay at any time. This is what medical science has accomplished and demonstrated.

When as a nurse I sat in workshops for counselling techniques, I observed the therapist very skillfully bring out many things from the deep shadows of the past. The patient became consciously aware of some specific hurt and trauma. He even sensed a return of the original, intense emotional involvement. I waited with keen anticipation for some vital and effective solution, but I saw the patient go home with an open wound and only a tranquilizer to mollify the hurt. My heart cried out, "Is there no way to relieve their pain?" Surely there has to be a better answer than a tranquilizer! Why, I have known some people who had been on pills of this kind for ten years.

To illustrate how startling it can be when something from the past is suddenly flashed into our conscious awareness, I will tell you my own personal experience. When I was a student nurse, I often returned to the hospital from Vancouver on the old interurban train. We had to be in by 10:15 p.m., so naturally most of the nurses were on the latest possible run. There was a certain conductor on that train who affected me very strangely. I couldn't figure it out. Every time he would come to get my ticket, something within me recoiled, and I felt a certain sickening revulsion toward him. I was very loathe to get on the train if I saw him there. I was nonplussed. I asked the Lord to show me what it was. Like a flash, one day the whole thing came before me:

When I was just a little girl travelling by train across Canada with my parents on our way to England, there had been a conductor who had frightened me very badly. I had been afraid to tell my mother. During the ensuing years it seemed to be forgotten — until some familiar characteristic of this present conductor thrust into my conscious awareness the terror of that early train experience.

Once I knew the source, I asked the Lord to wipe it from my mind and to help me realize objectively that there was no connection between the two men. If I hadn't known the Lord, I could not have continued to ride that train.

Through my own experience I realized that things from our past have an effect on our adult lives. We are largely the product of the pre-programming of our childhood, and this determines our adult reactions to certain stimuli in daily experiences.

Fear is a taught thing. A child learns that the stove is hot by parental teaching or painful experience. I grew up afraid of the dark. It was at night that the witches and goblins were out to get little girls. The night was not a friend; it was an enemy. As I grew older, if I had to be out after dark, I would take big long steps and whistle like a man, hoping to scare off any menace lurking in the shadows. I was afraid of the dark even after I was married. If my husband was out of town, fear would come upon me as cold terror at night.

The Lord showed me that this fear stemmed from my childhood. He healed those memories and enabled me to handle my fears.

"I sought the Lord and He heard me, and delivered me from *all* my fears" (Ps. 34:4).

But first of all, I had to face those fears knowledgeably in order to deal with them objectively.

Now, if medical science and psychiatry can reveal the experiences which caused the hurts, the trauma of the past which in turn makes us react as we do in our adult life, how much more can the Holy Spirit? The Scriptures tell us that He is the One

"...Who searches all things" (I Cor. 2:10).
"He searches the heart" (Rom. 8:27).
"All things are naked and open before the eyes of Him with whom we have to do" (Heb. 4:13).
"The Lord searches all hearts and understands all the imaginations of the thoughts" (I Chron. 28:9).

How beautiful it is to know that when the Holy Spirit reveals these hidden memories, it is to heal them and not to batter us with them. It is often necessary for the Lord to bring the hurtful things to the surface to heal them. Jesus said, "I am the Light of the world" (John 8:12) — and light reveals and exposes. "All things...are made manifest (or visible) by the Light" (Eph. 5:13). Jesus Christ is the One Who, in the very beginning of time, said: "Let there be light," and there was light. Light is energy, and His energy has not abated one iota — it is from eternity to eternity. There is no energy crunch in Him. He is radiant energy: the Light which not only reveals but also heals.

When I was a student nurse working in the emergency department, suddenly ambulances began bringing in maimed and mangled people. Soon the word followed: There had been a head-on train collision not far from the hospital. One patient was the waiter in the dining car who had been severely scalded when a boiler exploded. His skin was hanging in shreds and he was suffering intense shock. The medical treatment he received in those days illustrates the healing qualities of light.

He was laid on a bed, and his whole body was sprayed with a substance called tannic acid jelly. Then a canopy, lined with rows of electric light bulbs, was placed over him. The warm rays of the light congealed the tissues of the skin, forming a coating or scab over the burned area. This prevented the precious body plasma from leaking away.

When He Who is divine energy and light touches you, He will heal you. That's why, when you need healing, hidden or forgotten incidents are revealed to you. As we have noted, the roots of psychosomatic illness are not in the physical manifestations but are imbedded in the "psyche." If we only treat symptoms, the results are palliative — a cover-up.

Let us examine the word "psyche" from which we derive such words as "psychiatry" and "psychology." It is a Greek word translated in the Bible in two ways: soul and life. For instance, we find it used in Matthew 16:26 where it is rendered "soul".

"What shall it profit a man if he gain the whole world and lose his own soul?"

Luke 12:23 uses the same word to mean "life."

"The life is more than meat, and the body more than raiment."

There is something of intrinsic worth about that part of you which is absolutely, singularly you, the soul-life, the personality. God doesn't make carbon copies. You are unique, a separate entity, singularly you. He Who made every snowflake different didn't beggar Himself when He made each one of us distinct, and individually loved by Himself. The Psalmist said:

"You did knit me together in my mother's womb" (Psalm 139:13),

and even:
"Your eyes saw my unformed substance, and in Your book all the days of my life were written, before ever they took shape, when as yet there was none of them" (Ps. 139:16 Amplified).

In fact,
"He hath *chosen* us in Him before the foundation of the world, that we should be holy, and without blame before Him in love" (Eph. 1:4).

We have to say in the words of David, "Such knowledge is too wonderful for me" (Psalm 139:6).

He sees, He knows every hurt of your whole life, every deep festering wound buried deep within the "psyche" and He came to heal, to make you whole. How do I know? Because He said so. He stood in the synagogue one day in Nazareth and read these prophetic words from the book of Isaiah:

"He hath sent Me to heal the brokenhearted, to preach deliverance to the captives, and recovering of sight to the blind;"

and as so beautifully expressed in the Amplified Bible:

"To send forth delivered those who are oppressed — who are downtrodden, bruised, crushed and broken down by calamity" (Luke 4:18).

I remind you that He is the unchanging One (Hebrews 13:8). His radiant, healing energy can never be depleted. He is waiting to heal you. As you wait quietly, even now, in the Light of His matchless Presence, as His Word has been speaking to your heart, you can be healed. I have recounted to you my own experience of healing when the Holy Spirit flashed upon the screen of my memory the events of childhood which had caused such fear and insecurity and then He bathed and washed me clean with His healing love. You may be recoiling from the thought of some painful memory at this moment — don't bury it again. Ask the Lord Jesus to heal you. May I lead you in a simple prayer to help you reach out to touch Him for yourself?

"Lord Jesus, I am hurting deep inside. The memories are too painful for me. I cannot bear them. I believe Your Word which tells me that You bore our griefs and carried our sorrows (Isaiah 53:4). I ask You, Jesus, to heal me completely, not only of the memories but of their devastating effects upon my being. I rest in Your healing. I accept it in Your Name. Thank You, Jesus."

This is the beginning of your total healing. I suggest that by simple faith you rejoice in His deliverance and anticipate completion of His work in you.

CHAPTER SIX

DESTROYING THE CANKERWORM

When the Lord Jesus shines His light into the dark shadows of the past, He often exposes deep festering wounds. Many times during prayer for the healing of these hurtful memories I have had a picture in my mind, by the Spirit, of the actual healing process. I would like to describe it for you:

A waterfall of sparkling light descends into the depths of the wound. It separates and out of it comes a fine beam of concentrated light like a laser beam which cuts away all the dead tissue around the edges of wound. Then the waterfall cascades over it, washing out all the accumulated filth until only healthy pink flesh remains. Finally, the Hands of the Heavenly Surgeon appear and perform a delicate and perfect skin graft — until there is not even a scar remaining.

His healing is so complete that the memory will never hurt again. It will be as though it happened to someone else. You must not go digging around in the ashes to see if you can find any vestigial remains. I once heard a very pertinent saying:

"Fear knocked on the door; faith opened it and found nothing there."

Go on from here and walk into God's future for you with confidence and assurance. Do not look back. Keep your eyes on the goal.

You are now on the road to a whole new dimension of living. The next step is yours, and it is a decisive act of your will. It is to willingly let go the appendages and encumbrances of *resentment,* which have attached themselves to you through your hurt. Resentment masquerades in many different forms: bitterness, grudges, animosity, hatred, unforgiveness, self pity. These things eat like a cankerworm into every area of the being, causing physical illness, depression, spiritual oppression and social havoc. You have clutched them tightly to yourself too long. Now you must release them with open hand.

Excuse my rather homely illustration, but if you keep hanging on to resentment, it is like having a dead skunk under your house. You may scrub the house, spray it with deodorants, open all the windows to let the breezes blow through, but you will still have the smell. You have to get rid of the skunk!

Let us note the words of Jesus in John 12:25 as rendered by Wuest's literal translation:

"He who is fond of and loves his *soul life* is losing it: and he who is hating and disregarding his soul life in the sphere of this world with a view to life eternal is preserving it safe and unimpaired."

He is saying that if we cuddle and nurture all those negative things which come into the soulish area of our lives, we will lose. The joy of our Christian lives will be submerged by them. But if we will cast them away from us, not catering to them but hating them, we will surely win — we will come into wholeness. It is taking the emphasis off this life and placing it on that which is eternal. This is a very down-to-earth and practical principle of victorious living.

The trouble is that sometimes we want to hold on to our *resentments,* thinking that they will provide us with a crutch to lean on. Carol was just such a person. She had been desperately hurt in her marriage, and although there was a reconciliation, she said to me, "I have forgiven him, but I don't plan on forgetting." She felt a sort of comfort in knowing that she had something to clobber him with if he got out of line again. However, that *bitterness* rankled within her, and terrible migraine headaches became the order of the day. She finally realized the depth of this destructive force, and called on the Lord to help her cast it away and let it go. She seemed to come out of abject darkness into the bright sunlight. Even her appearance changed. Her marriage was healed, and her migraine headaches began to diminish perceptibly.

Self pity and the "poor me" attitude, if indulged in, will quickly become a way of life that is most destructive. We have heard of alcoholics and "workoholics", but there is also the "selfoholic." Sometimes it would seem that these people really enjoy their self pity, and the thought of living without it is unbearable. Many have been caught in a web which has lost them friends, family and health. Bob's second name was "Calamity". When I asked about his friends, he said, "I have none." It seemed as though it would be a long way up from the bottom, but when he was willing to take the focus of attention off himself and major on the greatness of the Lord Jesus, he then realized just how much he had going for him.

An *unforgiving spirit* is also a destructive force within us. Webster's definition of "forgiveness" is:

"To give up resentment against, to give up all claim to punish or exact penalty, to stop being angry, to cancel or remit a debt."

To forgive a person who has wronged you is a very comprehensive act, and a great deal depends upon it. We read in Matthew 6:12 the words we recite so often in prayer:

"Forgive us our debts, *as* we forgive our debtors."

In effect, we are praying that God will forgive us to the same degree we give forgiveness to others. It's a sobering thought. Jesus goes on in Matthew 6:14-15 with these serious words:

"For if ye forgive men their trespasses, your heavenly Father will also forgive you; but if ye forgive not men their trespasses, neither will your Father forgive your trespasses."

Does this mean that our salvation depends upon something *we* can do? No! Our initial forgiveness depends upon the Judicial act of the Cross of Jesus Christ, where "He Who knew no sin became sin for us." (I have paraphrased this from II Corinthians 5:21.) Our sins were judged at the Cross. The penalty has been paid once and for all. Jesus was not speaking to unbelievers but to His own disciples. He is telling them that an unforgiving spirit will destroy fellowship and communion with the Father, shutting out the Light, and plunging them into darkness, defeat and guilt.

How often I have seen this happen and heard people say, "I can't pray any more. It seems that God is so far away and my prayers just hit the ceiling. I have no joy in my life. Life has become dull and meaningless." As we seek for a reason, frequently the confession is: "But I can never forgive. The pain that person caused me is too great."

It is true that on our own we cannot forgive. It is when we are willing to let Jesus help us that we can be released, and then the free flow of fellowship will be restored, and the peace and joy in Him renewed.

We cannot really give forgiveness until we have experienced it. It is only when we understand the depths of His forgiveness in our lives that we can forgive. Mary was very young, and had suffered a deep hurt. One day she said to me, "If God has forgiven him, *who am I* that I should not forgive? Through this experience I have seen my own heart, that I always thought was so clean and free from impure motives. Only now do I appreciate how much God has forgiven me." She even thanked God for the experience which taught her the true meaning of forgiveness.

I want to make the steps to wholeness just as practical as I possibly can for you. The first one, as already mentioned, is that *by a decisive act of your will you give up all that resentment and self pity,* etc. Give it to God with finality. It is important that you vocalize these things. I am not teaching psychology, but it is psychologically beneficial, and necessary for you to "confess with your mouth" what you believe. The Bible clearly states:

"The tongue of the wise uses knowledge rightly" (Prov. 15:2) and "Death and life are in the power of the tongue" (Prov. 18:21).

I would like to help you in a prayer of release:

"Lord Jesus, I bow before You, realizing my deep need. I have clutched these resentments, all the self pity and bitterness to myself for so long that I do not know how to let them go, and they are destroying me. I ask You to help me now as I willingly open my clenched fists as a token of my decision to let them all go, once and for all. Help me not to clutch at them again. Help me to focus upon Your greatness and Your goodness from this day on. Thank You, Jesus. I believe You. Amen."

There is a second step which may be necessary: *If the person against whom you have held this resentment is aware of it, you may need to go to that one saying you forgive and have laid aside all bitterness.* It may be a parent or some other member of the family, and the feud may have become intolerable. Jesus said:

"Blessed are the peacemakers: for they shall be called the children of God" (Matt. 5:9).

Go gently, go kindly, go lovingly in the Name of Jesus. If that person has passed away, do not allow Satan to beat you with condemnation. Take it to Jesus and lay it at the Cross. Then leave it there.

I said that this step "may" be necessary. Let me clarify this by a warning: We must never confess anything that will hurt someone else, either directly or indirectly. Perhaps that person is not aware of the hurt or bitterness you feel. By confessing it to him, you will transfer your resentment and guilt to him. I have seen this happen many times, and I have seen deep hurts because of it. I will give you a little illustration from my own experience.

I received a phone call one day from a friend who said, "There is something I have to tell you. For a long time I have resented you terribly. I don't like the way you speak. I don't like the way you lead the songs. I really don't like anything about you!" This was all news to me — I never dreamed she felt this way. Then with a big sigh of relief she said, "Whew! do I ever feel better!"

"Well, I am glad you feel better," I said, when I could get my breath."I don't feel so good myself."

In Matthew 5:23-24 of the New International Version Bible Jesus said:

"If you are offering your gift at the altar and there remember that your brother has something *against you,* leave your gift there in front of the altar. First go, and be reconciled to your brother; then come and offer your gift."

The trouble is that we often read those verses backwards. If we have something against our brother, we go off to tell him so, when the thing we should do is pray for him. Jesus said that if our brother "has something against" us, if we have hurt him and he knows it, then we are to go to him and make it right. Much harm is done because we do not read Scripture correctly.

Another instance of misapplied confession was made clear to me when I counselled a young couple who were about to break up. The husband had sinned against his wife but had confessed it to God with deep repentance. Then some time later he felt he must also confess this to his wife — who was totally unaware of any such thing. The knowledge crushed her to the ground. Her heart was broken. It seemed that she could not find her way up out of the darkness of her hurt. Of what value was such a confession? What inestimable pain it caused! We must ask God for great wisdom and also for an understanding of the very essence of wisdom:

"The wisdom that comes from heaven is first of all pure; then peace-loving, considerate, submissive, full of mercy and good fruit, impartial and sincere" (James 3:17 N.I.V.).

There are two types of *resentment* which I would like to define. I call them "delayed resentment" and "immediate resentment." We have been dealing mainly with the "delayed" action type — which is the result of some painful experience of the past. But what do we do about "immediate resentment" when someone hurts us or hurts someone we love?

We are misunderstood, deceived or betrayed, and immediately we are on the defensive, our backs are up and the old churning begins deep within. If we allow it to simmer, we are in for trouble. What will we do? We must nip it in the bud. Jesus gives us the answer in Matthew 5:44:

"Pray for them which despitefully use you, and persecute you."

He gave us the greatest example of all when from the agony of the Cross He prayed:

"Father, forgive them, for they know not what they do" (Luke 23:34).

It was only when the Holy Spirit came on the day of Pentecost that the ones who crucified Jesus were made to understand that the One they had put to death was "both Lord and Christ" (Acts 2:36-37).

The trouble with us is that too often we are like James and John who were irked at the Samaritans who did not receive Jesus, so they said:

"Lord, wilt Thou that we command fire to come down from Heaven and consume them?"

But Jesus

"rebuked them and said, Ye know not what manner of spirit ye are of. For the Son of man is not come to destroy men's lives, but to save them" (Luke 9:55-56).

You see, God loves those persons who have hurt you. Jesus also died for them. If you pray for them in this light, you will no longer hate them. A fountain does not

"...send forth at the same place sweet water and bitter" (James 3:11).

55

Neither can you both love and hate at the same time. Remember that your bitterness does not hurt them — it hurts only you. *Pray!*

Beware Psychoanalysis

We have been talking about the wounds of the past and of childhood experiences. The question I have been asked is this: "If we ask the Holy Spirit to bring out those past hurts and nothing shows up, what do we do?" My answer is: We must not go digging for skeletons which may not be there. Do we or do we not believe God when we pray? There are two things I am going to suggest that you consider:

1) The Holy Spirit is all wisdom and He knows best what should be brought to the surface and what should not.

2) Maybe there is nothing there, and you need to learn to walk in the Spirit.

Now let us examine these more closely. I like to illustrate the first consideration from a very simple premise of first aid: If a person swallows a caustic poison which has already burned all the way down, we do not make him vomit because it would burn the second time as it came up again. The damage would be doubled. Therefore, the treatment is to *neutralize* the poison. As this is not a textbook on first aid, I am using this simply to illustrate my point.

When the Holy Spirit in His infinite wisdom does not bring anything to the surface, it may be to protect you from a hurt you could not bear. Therefore we do not keep on digging interminably, but we neutralize the pain with the healing balm of the Name of Jesus. The Song of Solomon in 1:3 tells us that "His Name is as ointment poured forth." It is not a mantra to be recited as some type of incantation. But by a simple prayer of faith, we bathe that person and all the unknown hurts with the Name of Jesus — which in the Hebrew means "salvation" — (safety and soundness). The angel said to Joseph:

"Thou shalt call His Name Jesus: for He shall *save* (heal and make whole) His people from their sins" (Matt. 1:21).

This is clearly exemplified in the story of a young woman who suffered a terrifying experience in hospital after the birth of her child. The incident had never been mentioned to the child, but as he grew up he had serious emotional problems. They may have been related to the thing which happened in his infancy. To project this horror into his conscious awareness now would have added an unbearable weight to that which he was already carrying in his subconscious mind. Therefore the prayer of faith was to neutralize all the "poison" by bathing the child in the healing Name of Jesus. God answered prayer and restored him to wholeness. We can trust the wisdom of our great God.

"O the depths of the riches both of the wisdom and the knowledge of God! How unsearchable are His judgments, and His ways past finding out!" (Rom. 11:33).

The second thing we mentioned is that there may be no hurtful experience to be exposed and you need to learn to walk in the Spirit. Let us be careful where we lay blame for our bitternesses and our defeatist attitude — it may be very close to home. The Bible says:

"Walk in the Spirit, and you shall not fulfil the lust of the flesh" (Gal. 5:16).

Sometimes the things which we battle in our daily personal lives — and for which we like to lay blame somewhere else — are simply what the Bible calls "the works of the flesh." There is a big long list of these given in Galatians 5:19-21. To walk in the Spirit means that the "fleshly desires" are crucified, left at the Cross, and now we are "under new management." The indwelling Spirit is our new "Boss." We do not cater any longer to something which is dead.

How to remain in victory

1) After your hurt is healed, and you have laid the resentments at the foot of the Cross, you must walk on into life. Do not withdraw or shut yourself away from further hurt by saying, "I'll never love again. I'll never trust again." Life is not a spectator sport. You can only touch life by being involved in life. You must share what you have received because you can only keep what you give away. You have been comforted that you

"...may be able to comfort them which are in any trouble, by the comfort wherewith you yourself have been comforted by God" (II Cor. 1:4).

And I would say in the words of Jesus, "Freely you have received, freely give" (Matt. 10:8).

2) You have "put off" an old way of life and "put on" the new life in Christ; *now* you must be continually "renewed in the spirit of your mind" (Eph. 4:23). You must reprogram your mind to a Bible "think." According to Romans 12:2 we are not to be

"...conformed to this world (or its pattern for living), but be *transformed* by the renewing of our minds..."

The word "transformed" suggests a totally new lifestyle. It is translated from the Greek "metamorphoo" from which our word "metamorphosis" is derived. The word means a change in form and character, as seen in that of the caterpillar into a butterfly. There is nothing in the butterfly which in any way resembles its former existence as a caterpillar. It is no longer interested in a diet of leaves when it can flit among the blossoms sipping the nectar.

The "transformed" child of God is a "new creature" with new interests, new desires, and a whole new way of life. (Note II Corinthians 5:17). He no longer goes crawling back to the old diet, whether the garbage of sensuality or godless philosophies, horoscopes or mysticism, resentment or self-pity. He now feeds into the computer of his mind the cleansing, faith-building truths of God's Word. Have you checked your diet lately?

CHAPTER SEVEN

THE IDENTITY OF ANGER

Each day when I am alone with the Lord for a little while it seems as though it is just He and I together. I realize that He is unique because He can be mine and I can claim Him as my own personal dearest Friend even though He is also the Friend of millions of other people. The Psalmist glimpsed the reality of this great truth when he said:

"Whither shall I go from Thy Spirit? Or whither shall I flee from Thy Presence?" (Psalm 139:7).

Let us not try to confine our God to a little box walled in by time and space. There are no boundaries to His presence with me nor to His knowledge of me. I am never left alone. I am never unnoticed (Psalm 139:1-3). May I urge you to take a few moments to read this portion of Scripture?

I pray now for you, my reader, that God will continue and complete the work that He has started in your life. I have asked that He will heal you and make you whole through His eternal Word.

"And this is the confidence that we have in Him, that if we ask anything according to His will, He hears us: and if we know that He hears us, whatsoever we ask, we know that we have the petitions that we desired of Him" (I John 5:14-15).

The next thing we must consider in our progress toward healing and wholeness is that devastating inner conflict: ANGER. It is a deadly tool in the hands of Satan. I have counselled many people whose spiritual lives are ravaged by the effects of anger and hostility. How do we handle this impelling force which has such potential to destroy?

We must understand that anger is an emotion. It has to do with the soulish part of me — where I hurt and how I feel deep inside. Emotions are an integral part of the whole person. My emotional self is as vital as every other area — I am an indivisible and composite unity. Therefore the way I react to these emotions manifests itself throughout the whole "me".

Emotions are very much a part of the personality, or that which identifies me as being "me". When God "saves" us and we become "new creatures in Christ Jesus," He doesn't put us on an assembly line and turn us all out identically alike. I am still "me" with the same identifying personality. But *now* I have a new life within me — the resurrection Life of Christ which enables me to overcome the old drives and appetites in order to live to the greatest of my potential for Him.

We must always be aware of this: each individual is singular in his own right. My husband and I are very different. He is very practical and not too moved by sentiment — these are some of the qualities which drew me to love and respect him, for I am just the opposite. During the years we were raising our family, every once in a while I would get some bright ideas (I thought!)

"Honey," I would say, "I've got it all figured out how we could alter this house," He'd turn that certain look on me which wives know so well, but I would continue undaunted — "We could remove this wall and put it over there, and put these stairs on the other side," — and then I would see the dollar signs forming in his practical mind, and hear: "Have you any idea what that would cost?" Well, I hadn't given that a thought. Then he would bring me back to earth by asking me such a mundane question as: "And what do you think that would do to the beams and supports of this house?" There went my impractical dream. It could be catastrophic if we were exactly alike.

Now emotions are as necessary as the mainspring of a watch without which the watch could not function. The word "emotion" comes from the Latin "emovere" which means "to move out." Without this motivating force we would be apathetic and accomplish nothing. It is how emotions are controlled, disciplined and used which determines whether the response will be beneficial or destructive.

Regarding the emotion of anger, the Bible says:

"He who is slow to anger is better than the mighty, and he who rules his spirit than he who takes a city" (Prov. 16:32).

It does not say that anger in itself is essentially wrong. We read in Ephesians 4:26:

"Be ye angry, and sin not. Let not the sun go down upon your wrath."

or in other words:

"In your anger do not sin: Do not let the sun go down while you are still angry, and do not give the devil a foothold" (N.I.V.).

We must know how to handle anger lest we fall into Satan's trap.

I want to liken this emotion of anger to a river tumbling harmlessly down a mountain side. When flood season comes the water is whipped into a furious torrent tearing out everything in its path. Uncontrolled, it is bent on destruction. Men have devised a way to harness this mighty force for good. By building a dam they channel the water through the penstocks into the power house where it turns the huge turbines, producing electrical energy to bring light and power to our cities. The river, controlled and directed, is now useful and beneficial.

When all that pent-up anger within us is harnessed and brought under the control of the Holy Spirit, the energy generated may be released in positive and productive ways.

Uncontrolled anger is on a collision course. We will consider four possible consequences: 1) Leads to acts of vengeance. 2) Brings regret and remorse. 3) Affects the whole person. 4) Is a hindrance to spiritual growth.

1) *It could lead me to commit acts of vengeance.* Jesus put it this way:

"Everyone who continues to be angry with his brother, or harbors malice toward him, shall be liable to and unable to escape the punishment imposed by the court" (Matt. 5:22 Amplified).

Jesus knew that pent-up anger may finally explode into acts of vengeance which will bring a charge against me, and I will have to pay the sentence imposed by the court. This happened to my friend, Pete. He would get so angry that it would boil up within him like steam under pressure. One day it broke loose. In his unreasoning fury without thought of the consequences, he set out to "get even". He was charged with a criminal offence and paid the penalty.

How many highway accidents are the result of anger? There was an argument in the family and hot words were spoken. Gerry's temper flared and he rushed from the house. Jumping into his car, his hands clenching the wheel, he floored the accelerator. Blinded by rage, he never saw the other car pull into the intersection. There were screeching brakes, a grinding crash — and two people lay dead in the wreckage.

2) *Anger out of control brings inevitable regret and remorse in its wake.* A good illustration of this is found in the Old Testament book of Esther. King Ahasuerus was "enraged" (1:12 Amplified) because his wife refused to put on a performance in the banquet room before his drunken guests. His anger "burned within him" and he expelled her from his home and his kingdom. In chapter two we read that when "his wrath was appeased he remembered Vashti," but it was too late — the royal decree had been sealed. All his regret and remorse could not undo what he had done in a fit of anger.

Pete, too, was inconsolable. He buried his head in his hands and sobbed, "If only I hadn't done it. I was too mad to think. I just wanted to get even." What remorse!

3) *Anger, uncontrolled, affects the whole person.* The body reacts to a fit of rage by pouring adrenalin into the blood stream. This internal secretion has been called "a hormone for emergencies" because it increases the heart rate and raises the blood pressure. This sudden speeding up of the

circulatory system may cause sufficient stress to trigger a heart attack or stroke. (It is interesting to note here that the words "anger" and "angina" are derived from the same Greek word "anchone"!)

The effects on the digestive system can be equally dramatic because "the rush of adrenalin suspends the gastro-intestinal activities to shift more blood into the muscular area where it is needed for fight or flight."* The consequences of continual emotional crises during or following meals can cause ulcers.

The principles of the Bible are so plain and clear:

"A calm and undisturbed mind and heart are the life and health of the body. But envy, jealousy and anger are as rottenness of the bones" (Prov. 14:30 Amplified).

Job has been considered by many scholars to be the oldest book in the Bible, and written there we find this statement:

"Vexation and rage kill the foolish man; jealousy and indignation slay the simple" (Job 5:2 Amplified).

Through medical statistics we understand that ninety percent of the illnesses known to man cannot touch the person who has peace of mind. It is further known that seventy-five percent of all prescriptions written by doctors are to treat nervous disorders. The Bible again in its straight-forward way has tersely stated:

"A merry heart doeth good like a medicine" (Prov. 17:22).

I have found that God's Rx works the best.

4) *The fourth adverse result of uncontrolled anger is the hindrance to spiritual growth.* I would like to quote from the Wuest translation of James 1:19-20:

"Let every person be quick to hear, slow to speak, slow with respect to anger, for man's wrath does not bring about that which is righteous in God's sight."

He is speaking here about the "unbridled tongue" (verse 26). The words which spew forth from the lips in the heat of passion actually impede my Christian growth. They defeat me, discourage me, and lay guilt upon me. These hasty words can never be recalled. The ripples continue on and out to the very perimeter of my life, hurting others, and bringing great reproach upon the Name of our Lord Jesus.

I want to digress at this point to say a few words to that one who may be asking, "But who can have peace of mind in this troubled society?"

Physiology and Anatomy by Greisheimer & Blount

First, "peace" comes from a relationship with God through our Lord Jesus Christ (Rom. 5:1). Then the constancy of "peace" is a gift from Jesus to His children (John 14:27). Therefore it is not dependent upon outward circumstances. The practical demonstration of this peace in our daily lives is found in the admonition of Paul given in Philippians 4:6-7. I would like to quote this passage from the Living Bible:

"Don't worry about anything: instead pray about everything; tell God your needs and don't forget to thank Him for the answers. If you do this you will experience God's peace, which is far more wonderful than the human mind can understand. His peace will keep your thoughts and your hearts quiet and at rest as you trust in Christ Jesus."

Then, there may be those who say, "There is nothing in my life to be merry about." Let me remind you that "happiness" is also a relationship. The Psalmist says, "Happy is the people whose God is the Lord" (Ps. 144:15).

Although I cannot pursue this topic in depth here, I would like to suggest to my reader that you sit down with your Bible and concordance and make a little personal study of the word translated "blessed" in the New Testament. This word literally means "happy". Such a study will help to give you a whole new outlook.

We return to the subject of "anger" and refer to the exhortation of Scripture:

"The servant of the Lord must not be quarrelsome, fighting and contending" (II Tim. 2:24 Amplified).

In Galatians 5:20 "anger" is identified as one of the "works of the flesh". In Colossians 3:8 we are adjured by Paul to "put off anger" — to get rid of it.

I struggled with these verses for many years. My constant plea was, "But how do I do it?" I would bow in defeat time after time lamenting, "I guess I'm different. It doesn't work for me. I'm just stuck with this rotten temper." But when God led me into an understanding of myself through His Word, then into His provision for my "inner healing", He opened for me the way, at last, to victorious living.

I learned that we must know and identify what we are fighting in order to deal with it objectively. Paul puts it this way:

"I do not run uncertainly — without definite aim. I do not box as one beating the air and striking without an adversary" (I Cor. 9:26 Amplified).

When we can identify and pigeon-hole the enemy, we can strike him a death blow.

During my years of personal counselling I have uncovered and identified nine different types of anger insidiously at work in the inner being. I have given each one a name to help you relate to them and understand them. This is not an exhaustive list. I will simply list and illustrate them first, and then we will give direct and practical help for each.

Projected Anger

This is the kind that homes in like a guided missile toward a particular person.

a) It may be found in a *parent-child relationship*. The parent sees manifested in the child some of his own despised personality characteristics and the child becomes a target of intense animosity. This works two ways: there is some personality trait in the parent that the child doesn't like, and when he sees the same thing surfacing in his own life he blames the parent who passed it on to him. Sometimes what would seem to be an innocuous remark such as: "You are just like your mother (or dad)" is sufficient to trigger strong and bitter emotions. The child's anger is projected toward the offending parent.

I found this type of anger demonstrated in a mother and daughter who came for counselling. Gertie, the mother, came first. She told me that her teenage daughter riled her so badly she was desperate to know what to do. She said, "Sue is such a lovely girl that I don't understand why I have this intense irritation." After a time of discussion and prayer, I asked Gertie if she thought Sue would come to see me.

She came, and when I opened the door to her I found myself facing a replica of the mother. They were like two peas in a pod except for the few years difference in age between them. As we talked I soon recognized that the similarity was not just in appearance. Sue told me of her own personality conflicts. It was almost a repetition of what Gertie had told me about herself. They were both the same, hating themselves and hating each other — and not knowing why. When the whole thing was opened up to them, it was a revelation. They were able to see it objectively, and with prayerful guidance a beautiful relationship was established between them.

Sally's problem illustrates another facet of anger in the parent-child relationship. Sally was guilty of child abuse. Inflamed by hatred and uncontrollable rage, she would beat her child mercilessly even when he was just an infant. She was so afraid of herself that she pleaded for help. The Holy Spirit in His infinite faithfulness showed us areas of terrible hurt and trauma in Sally's own childhood. She wept bitterly as she recalled the experiences. Until these memories were healed and all the anger associated with them cleansed, she could not relate to her son in love. We first had to destroy the roots. Taking each specific experience, we prayed for healing in the Name of Jesus. We bathed those areas one by one in His healing love until she knew that He had touched her.

The Holy Spirit exposes that He might heal, and His healing power is complete.

b) Sometimes we see "projected anger" *in the marriage relationship.* Those little habits and differences we were unconcerned about in the rosy glow of courtship become giants in our path when we settle down to the humdrum of wedded life. Irritations erupt in anger and hostility. We cry out in despair, "Where is our beautiful dream?" Vainly we try to put one another into our own comfortable mold.

This tendency to try to make plastic saints of one another has sometimes become the butt of good humor — as in this little classic from our own experience: In the toast to the bride when my husband and I were married the comment was made: "Joan has three things in her mind tonight — the aisle, the altar and him. Put it all together and it says, "I'll alter him!" I will confess there were times I tried, but it didn't work. And I'm glad. If I put him in my mold he wouldn't be himself, and it was "himself" I fell in love with.

c) There is the anger that is projected toward *someone who has caused us hurt.* We may have brought it into a quiescent state, but should we cross paths with that person, it flares up within us. Such was the case with Andy. He could handle his anger well if he never had to see Bruce, so he went out of his way to avoid a personal confrontation. But sometimes Bruce was just there — part of the same group — and instinctively that old anger would begin to churn.

d) There is yet another subtle form which is *the result of a traumatic experience in the past.* It is buried deep in the subconscious. The ensuing years may have covered it up. Then suddenly it is thrust into the conscious memory by what would appear to be an irrelevant circumstance.

This is well illustrated in my earlier story of meeting a conductor on the interurban train who stirred an instant revulsion within me. Each time he collected my ticket I felt the same hostility, until there flashed back into my memory the picture of myself on a train travelling across Canada with my family many years ago. I was a small child, and the conductor on that train had frightened me badly. This present man looked so much like the other that it awakened within me the old anger and fear which had been buried for so long.

Explosive Anger

This "explosive anger" is the type which can be ignited by situations arising in the course of an ordinary day. These people seem to live on the rim of a volcano — they never know when something will trigger a blow-up. This puts great strain on the family who must learn to handle them with kid gloves. In the morning Mother will have to caution the children, "Watch out for Dad today. Be quiet and handle him carefully — he could blow any time." Or Dad may have to say, "Look, kids, this is Mother's bad day.

Take it easy and stay out of her way. Keep the dog out of the kitchen, and don't you dare spill the milk on her clean tablecloth." The whole family pussy-foots around in fear.

This type of situation can become a volatile problem in the work force. When I was counselling in occupational health, I found that one such person could shatter the cooperative efforts of a whole departmental team. Because it is possible that this person may be suffering from an underlying illness or disease, I always suggest a complete medical check-up to rule out any hidden health problem.

I remember Shirley, who daily had all her fellow-employees on tenterhooks. We found that she had a serious alcohol problem in the home. She never told anyone about it, but she came to work each day burdened down with anxiety that she couldn't dump. It clouded all her thinking and caused her to be short-tempered and irritable.

Smoldering Anger

Smoldering anger is subtle, lying beneath the surface and hiding behind a smile. It is like a fifth column driven underground working its way insidiously into the very fabric of the inner being.

The person may feel that he really has it under control, until it pops up at some unexpected moment. Perhaps its appearance is prompted by the presence of someone whom he dislikes intensely. Quickly he hides behind a facade of friendliness, but he is aware of the angry churning inside. It is like an underground fire in a peat field that can smolder for years. There is always a fear that it will come to the surface and be revealed. These people are particularly susceptible to psychosomatic illness.

When I first met Peg I was impressed by her warmth and friendliness. She was always joking, laughing and seemed to be the life of the party. Although she maintained this continual ebullience, she began to complain of vague illnesses. She underwent numerous medical tests which revealed very little. After we had had some talks, I realized the depth of her anger. Behind the stories she related with such humor were hostile barbs filled with the poison of her anger. This poison was filtering into every part of her being. It was something that didn't show up on an X-ray or in a test tube — but it was there.

Inborn Anger

This inborn anger manifest itself in a sense of failure, worthlessness and hopelessness. It is directed against the person's self because he never "made it". It spills over in anger against family, society and "a God Who never gave him a chance."

It results in a hatred of oneself — appearance and personality. I read recently in a newspaper article that psychiatrists have uncovered what they feel may be a new disease. They call it "dysmorphophobia" — a feeling by normal-looking people that they are ugly. I have counselled children, teenagers and older folk who suffer this way. They brood over their supposed "ugliness." They disqualify themselves. There develops a terrible inner hostility which has sometimes led to suicide.

Not very long ago I heard some startling statistics given by a member of the suicide squad at a local hospital. She said that in the lower mainland of this province of British Columbia there were about one hundred suicide attempts each month and that these mainly involved young people. It was estimated that only about six percent would recover. We have seen some who lived — but with irreparable brain damage.

"Inborn anger" originates early in life, at birth, or even before birth. Jenny was a twin. Her sister, born first, received all the attention because the mother hadn't wanted two babies. Jenny was a surprise package that was neither expected nor desired. From Day One she had to fight for her identity and place in the family. In our counselling sessions she spilled out her anger toward all involved, including God Who allowed it to happen and herself, the helpless victim.

When I met Jenny she was in despair. Her hostility was making terrible inroads into her marriage. I offered to help her but she only muttered, "No one can help *me*." I simply left the door open for her, and one day she phoned, pleading, "Can I talk with you?" The first thing we discovered that day was: She didn't know Jesus. To be "without Christ" is to be "without hope" (Ephesians 2:12). She gladly received Him as her personal Saviour, and then we had a base of operations from which to work to bring her into total healing.

Frustrated Anger

"Frustrated anger" is what a person feels who is caught in a trap and there is no way up or out. He may gripe and complain; he may even scream out his anger, but the walls of his prison are impregnable. Let me give you some explicit examples which I have encountered. At this point I will simply state the problems.

a) A seemingly impossible *marital situation*. There was Vera who felt locked into a problem. She had married her husband in good faith. She loved him. He has returned recently from one of his periodic business trips to his home country and informed her that he was supporting a *de facto* wife and their child in his homeland. He stated that this was culturally acceptable and that although she, his legal Canadian wife, was torn with hurt and anger, there was nothing he could do to change the situation.

b) An impossible *job situation*. It was Terry's first job. She needed the experience and the money. But she hated it. It was monotonous and boring. She was the waste basket for the older employees. She couldn't stand any of them.

c) A parent faced with the endless *care of a helpless, deformed or brain-damaged child.* One such parent said to me, "As far as I can see ahead, there is nothing but this day after day."

d) The constant *care of an elderly senile parent.* "Mother has lived with us for years," a woman said. "We couldn't put her in a nursing home now. But she is so impossible! We can't leave her alone for a minute lest she fall or leave the stove on or some such thing. We are at the end of our rope."

e) A young mother with several pre-school children. "I'm caught in a trap of diapers, dishes and screaming kids," she wails. "Is there no way out?"

f) *Some one cut down* in his prime by accident or an incapacitating illness. He cries out in despair, "Why did God let this happen to me?"

Now these are just a few of the problems of angry frustration which have been presented to me — there are numerous others.

Peripheral Anger

This doesn't touch a person directly, but is on the periphery of his life. It is the indignation and outrage one feels toward the seeming injustice of the social system in which he lives. Whenever I pass through the skid road area in our town and see the aimless youths staggering along the streets befuddled and incoherent with alcohol and drugs, anger rises within me towards those who propagate the stuff and make merchandise of men's souls.

It is the anger we feel toward the shops which peddle pornography, the schools which teach godless philosophies, and the television programs which exploit our kids. Possibly it is similar to the anger which Jesus felt when He drove the thieves and money changers from the temple.

Vengeful Anger

Vengeful anger is an overwhelming desire to get back at someone, to lay blame, and to cause another to suffer as we have.

It may stem from any of the previous angers we have mentioned. I have cited for you elsewhere the roots of a vengeful spirit which the Holy Spirit exposed in the heart of one who had been betrayed by her best friend. That friend had become an enemy. Every time she saw her "friend" this anger rose to gigantic proportions. "I want to see her suffer as I have. Why should she be laughing? Why should she go free? Why shouldn't she pay for the hurt she has caused?" This desire for revenge festered like a boil within her.

Rebellious Anger

I have found this type of anger expressed by young people who have been brought up in Christian homes and in the church. They feel that the beliefs of their parents have been foisted upon them. They are not sure of the validity of these beliefs in today's world where the principles of the Bible are being torn down and maligned by the schools, the media, and socially accepted mores. In some instances they have not seen the living proof in their homes. It seems that there is a disparity between what they see and what they hear.

One young person felt that it was all a pretence. Another said to me, "My parents want me to be a Christian and go their way so they can proudly say, 'Look at the good job we did of raising our son!' They have to keep up appearances."

Ken was one who was champing at the bit to get out from under the restraints of home and church. He told me his position was untenable. He was living two lives. While at school he followed the crowd. "They never even guessed I went to church," he said. While at church he *acted* according to the accepted norm there. "They never guessed either," he told me. "I fooled them all."

He respected his parents. He knew they lived what they believed, but he didn't want their faith. He felt he was caught in a trap, but because he didn't want to hurt his parents, he kept up his little game. One day he couldn't face it any longer. He walked out of school at lunch time and disappeared with his old jalopy. His parents, fearing foul play, were distraught. They had no idea of his conflict. But they called their church to pray. One week later Ken phoned home — he was fifteen hundred miles down the road. This is the story he told:

"I was sick, alone and broke. My gas tank registered only one-quarter full. It was raining so hard I could hardly see through the windshield, but I kept on driving. Suddenly I knew I was running away from a God I didn't know. I had never given Him a second thought. In my despair I cried out: 'O God, I need You. I need to know if You are real. Please come into my life and save me. Jesus, here I am — take me. I'm yours. I give my life to You.'

"At that moment Jesus came into my life for the first time. The tears streamed down my face and between the tears and the rain, I couldn't see a thing. The Lord must have driven that car the last four hundred miles to my aunt's home where I could stay. I knew my old car could never go four hundred miles on a quarter tank of gas — it had to be a miracle."

Ken touched God *for himself* that day.

I have also seen rebellious anger manifested in people to whom God has spoken about uncommitted areas in their lives. They want to align themselves with Jesus as their Saviour but not as their Lord. They are continually on the defensive and ready to fight if someone touches that sore spot. John said, "I knew I wasn't right with God. I fought Him on every count. I wore a mask — no one knew how far my heart was from God. One day He showed me the anger of my rebellion. He broke me, and falling at

His feet, I gave Him my all. I am a happy man for the first time in thirty years."

Suppressed Rebound Anger

This anger, the last type I will mention, was brought to my attention by a medical doctor who was present at one of my seminars. This is how he expressed it:

"Could I proffer the suggestion of another destructive form of anger? Suppressed rebound anger — that which one feels guilty about but cannot absolve oneself of — can turn around to be anger directed against himself, and has serious inner disruption."

I am so grateful for this further enlightenment. Any one of these angers, if not resolved, turns inward to guilt — one of the chief saboteurs of the whole person.

CHAPTER EIGHT

MASTERY OR MISERY?

Now that the various types of anger have been identified and described, the next thing we must do is learn how to bring them under control. There are three alternatives we may choose in our handling of anger: 1) We can vent it. 2) We can bury it. 3) We can face it.

1) *We can vent it.* We can give vent to it — let it blow, with the sparks flying where they may, and everybody in the line of fire running for cover. This method would seem to be totally destructive. As Jesus said in Matthew 5:22, we may find ourselves facing a charge in court.

In an effort to resolve marital conflicts, George and Alice had attended a group therapy session. There were several couples seated in a circle, and each couple was given the opportunity to verbalize their animosities toward each other before every one. After this session George and Alice came to me and were hurting desperately.

"How did it work?" I asked.

"It was the most terrible experience," George responded. "We lashed out at one another, exposing the most personal things, until we were both screaming and crying."

"And how did you feel, Alice?" I queried.

"I have never felt so low in all my life," she said. "I came away feeling there was no way we could ever mend this marriage now."

Their anger had been vented, but it produced a harvest of bitterness and hatred.

2) *We can bury it.* We can bury our anger, smother it, ignore it, pretend it isn't there — and go about living behind a mask of guilt and fear. As the anger seethes within, we may mutter through clenched teeth, "Oh, dear, I'm a Christian. I'm not supposed to get mad. I mustn't let on how I feel."

So gritting our teeth a little harder, we put on a smile which may fool everyone but ourselves. We know that we are phoney. We cover it up in one area simply to find it popping up somewhere else in numerous little irritations which drag us into constant defeat.

3) *We can face it.* We can admit that we have a problem, get it out into the open, face up to it, uncover its roots and expose them to the healing

light of Jesus Christ. This is the route I pray you will choose to go. And by the help of the Holy Spirit, I want to lay it out before you in the most simple and practical way, step by step.

Before dealing with each individual anger, I want to consider with you some positive principles which will cover all aspects in general. Three basic headings will give you consecutive steps to follow: 1) Discover what it is you are fighting. 2) Allow the roots of your anger to be exposed. 3) Commit that area of your life to Christ.

1) *Discover what it is you are fighting.* a) We must know and understand what and who we are fighting. b) We must know the enemy's tactics. c) We must know our weapons and be skilled in their use.

a) *We must know and understand what and who we are fighting.* Some new Christians are shattered to find that after their conversion their problems seem to be compounded. They must be prepared for this. We are in a battle, and we do have an enemy. Of course he doesn't bother us too much when we're on his side, but when we defect and align ourselves with Jesus, Satan directs all his venom against us. We are at war against the forces of evil, and we are exhorted in II Timothy 2:3 to "endure hardness as good soldiers of Jesus Christ," and again in I Timothy 6:12 to "fight the good fight of faith."

b) *We must know the enemy's tactics.* The Bible also gives us a clear understanding of his strategy so that we "are not ignorant of his devices" (II Corinthians 2:11), and we know that "he goes about as a roaring lion seeking whom he may devour" (I Peter 5:8). He also masquerades as "an angel of light" (II Cor. 11:14). Through Ephesians 6:12 we are given to understand his extreme subtlety:

> "We wrestle not against flesh and blood, but against principalities and powers, against the rulers of the darkness of this world (that is, demonic spirit forces), against spiritual wickedness (even) in high places."

This is not a physical conflict. It is waged in the realm of the spirit.

Sometimes we may think that when we are in prayer and worship, enjoying the Presence of the Lord, there is no way Satan can attack us. But this is not so. He slips unbidden into our closet of prayer to plant a thought of accusation or condemnation. He is aptly called "the accuser of the brethren" (Rev. 12:10). That is why we *must* know the Word of God and be able to come against the enemy immediately with the absolute:

> "There is therefore *now* no condemnation to them which are in Christ Jesus" (Romans 8:1).

He will come as "an angel of light" putting thoughts into our minds to lure us into some cul-de-sac where we will be vulnerable to his lies. Again, by knowing God's Word, we will be able to recognize the cunning voice of Satan. The Voice of our true Shepherd never harasses nor harangues; He never tells us to do anything that is opposed to His character or to the principles of His Word.

June thought it was the Lord Who had spoken to her one day and told her that her husband had been unfaithful to her. When she found it was true, her torment and despair were unbearable.

"Did this happen before he became a Christian?" I asked.

"Oh, yes, it did."

"Has he been true to you since his conversion?"

'Yes, I know he has."

"If you had known the Word of God," I said, "you would have realized that it was the subtle voice of Satan you heard, and you could have cast it from you."

"But it was a revelation," June declared.

"It is impossible for God to deny His own character," I told her. "He has promised those who bow at the Cross and receive forgiveness in the Name of Jesus that 'their sins and iniquities I will remember *no more*' (Hebrews 10:17). How can God tell you something that He has wiped off the slate, buried and forgotten? It is Satan who condemns and torments."

As we prayed, the Lord Jesus Who has "all power in Heaven and in earth" (Matt. 28:18) released June from the bondage put upon her by the enemy. She accepted her husband as the new man God had made of him.

Don't expect Satan to fight fairly — he will sneak up on you when you are tired and discouraged. Or he will snipe at you from his place of darkness after you have enjoyed a particular time of blessing in the Lord. These are his tactics.

Jesus went this route before us. He understands. He has "suffered being tempted" (Heb. 2:18), and "was in all points tempted like as we are, yet without sin" (Heb 4:15). Mark records in his Gospel that "immediately" after the glorious experience at the Jordan when "the heavens opened" and Jesus saw "the Spirit like a dove descending upon Him", and "a voice from Heaven" spoke, affirming His unique identity, *immediately* there followed forty days of suffering under a constant barrage from Satan. When Jesus was weak from hunger — as Luke tells us — Satan increased his artillery fire, coming against Jesus with his subtle insinuations, flagrant debate and outright bribery. Yes, our Lord Jesus has been there, and He is our great High Priest "touched with the feeling of our infirmities" (Hebrews 4:15).

c) *We must know our weapons and be skilled in their use.* We must put on the "whole armor of God" as laid out for us in Ephesians 6:13-17. The Bible is most explicit. It states:

"The sword of the Spirit . . . is the Word of God" (Eph. 6:17).

And in Revelation 12:11 we are told that:

"They overcame him (Satan) by the blood of the Lamb, and by the word of their testimony; and they loved not their lives unto the death."

Let me remind you that these weapons are specific weapons for specific purposes. When I was a nurse in training, we had no effective drugs to combat certain infections. Then penicillin, hailed as the miracle drug, came on the scene. It was a specific agent to fight specific infections and it worked. The Bible assures us that "the weapons of our warfare are not carnal" (or of the flesh). They are specific weapons for spiritual warfare and

"... mighty through God to the pulling down of strongholds; casting down imaginations... and bringing into captivity every thought to the obedience of Christ" (II Cor. 10:4-5).

Are you having difficulty with impure thoughts, imaginings and fantasies? You have adequate weapons for such combat. Do you know how to use these weapons against the enemy? We are told to submit ourselves to God and then "resist the devil, and he will flee" from us (James 4:7).

Now I used to think that meant I had to resist him physically by digging in my heels, tensing every muscle and yelling at him — but he never budged one inch. He wasn't afraid of my scuffling. Then I learned the meaning of that word "resist". It means "to hold over against". No longer do I now flail about aimlessly and ineffectively. I take my Sword and say: "Satan, I hold over against you this fact: According to God's eternal Word, you were defeated at the Cross of Jesus Christ when He triumphed over you and made an open show of you" (Col. 2:15). Satan slinks off like a whipped cur before the "It is written..." of the Word of God.

Jesus Himself gave us the perfect demonstration of the use of "the Sword of the Spirit" during His temptation in the wilderness. Each time He came against Satan with "It is written...." Even when Satan cunningly quoted the Scripture but twisted its meaning, Jesus felled him with another Scripture which brought it into balance. Thereby He taught us how essential it is to be "rightly dividing the word of truth" (II Timothy 2:15). The Bible does not vitiate itself; it does not deprive itself of its efficiency.

Perhaps you feel weak and helpless and the sword seems too big and heavy for you. Ah, but Jesus didn't leave you to struggle alone. He sent the Holy Spirit to "guide you into all truth" (John 16:13), to "teach you all things" (14:26), and to provide "dunamis" (the power and ability) to get this job done (Acts 1:8).

"I am a born-again Christian," someone said to me recently. "But I am not Spirit-filled."

"I would like to know why not," I replied. "Jesus has made all provision for you. Have you asked Him? He promised to give to all who ask (Luke 11:13). What are you waiting for? It is the command of Scripture:

"Be filled with the Spirit" (Eph. 5:18).

I sometimes say, "Get with it!" to the hesitant and fearful. As a child of God this gift is your rightful heritage (Acts 2:38).

2) *Allow the roots of your anger to be exposed.* After discovering and understanding what we are fighting, the next step we must take is to ask the Lord Jesus, by His Holy Spirit, to expose the roots of our anger — to bring before our conscious memory those hurtful experiences from the past that they may be dealt with and healed.

In Isaiah 51:1 the Lord is speaking to all those "that follow after righteousnesss" and "seek the Lord". He is telling them to "look unto the rock whence you are hewn, and to the hole of the pit whence you are dug." Look back to your beginning!

In Psalm 139 David exclaimed:

"Lord, You know all about me. You even know my thoughts, and the words I haven't yet spoken. You know every step I have taken. Why, Lord, You saw me before I was born and while I was being formed in my mother's womb. There's no way I can ever get away from your knowledge of me nor Your presence with me."

I have paraphrased these words in order to pin-point each thought.

Jesus knew all about Nathanael before they ever met (John 1:47-48). He knew all about the Samaritan woman, and she went into the city proclaiming: "Come, see a man which told me all things that ever I did: is not this the Christ?" (John 4:29).

And Jesus knows all about you too, my friend. He knows your name and where you live. He knows all the pain and hurt which, locked away unresolved in the subconscious mind, has programmed you to hostility and anger. He knows and He can put His finger on it, bring it out of the dark shadows and wash it clean. He will walk back with you through the past; He will come into each situation and bathe it with His healing power. When Jesus gets the roots out, His surgery is complete. Not even a scar remains to remind you. You do not need to keep going back over it looking for some minute shred of evidence. You must now

"...forget those things which are behind and press toward the mark for the prize of the high calling of God in Christ Jesus" (Phil. 3:13-14).

The day I knelt before the Lord in my living room and He exposed the roots of my personal battle with inferiority complex I cried out in anguish, "Oh, Lord Jesus, heal me!" He did exactly what I asked Him to — He healed me. I have never looked back since except to recount my experience to help others. There is no hurt now. It's like an acutely inflamed appendix — once it's out it can't hurt any more; neither can it pour poison into the system. It's gone — finished with.

Be specific in your prayer. Honor the Lord by praying according to His greatness. His promise is to

"...supply all your need *according to* His riches in glory by Christ Jesus" (Phil. 4:19).

Why do you ask for small things? Blind Bartimaeus could have asked for a seeing-eye dog to help him around, but before him stood the Creator of the universe, and he asked in accordance: "Lord, that I might receive my sight." He got what he asked for.

I could have drawn back in horror as the Lord opened to view those things which I had buried for so long. I could have prayed, "Oh, Lord, cover it up quickly. I can't bear to look upon it." But I knew that wasn't good enough — I asked for total healing, and this is what He gave me.

3) *Make a total commitment of every aspect of anger to Jesus Christ.* The third step is a very decisive one which we must take: a total commitment of every aspect of the anger Jesus has exposed to Him — once and for all. God always demands some effort on our part. Because He respects human dignity, He gives each one something to do. Jesus told the blind man, "Go and wash in the pool of Siloam," and He told the lepers, "Go show yourselves to the priest."

In view of God's mercies so freely bestowed upon us, Paul exhorts us to

"...make a decisive dedication of our bodies — presenting all our members and faculties — as a living sacrifice, holy and well-pleasing to God" (Romans 12:1 Amplified).

You must perform a specific act, something *concrete* to bind this commitment much as one does by "signing on the dotted line." This little exercise will help you: Hold up to the Lord your clenched fists while you say:

"Lord, these fists represent the anger and bitterness which I have held so tightly for too long. It is destroying me, Lord. I desperately need Your help. I release it all to You *now,* and by Your grace I will not take it back again."

At this point, open your hands wide, turn them over, drop the anger — as it were. Then give Him an offering of praise and worship for His faithfulness until you sense the witness of His peace in your heart.

Then if Satan tries to put this anger on you again, you can say: "Satan, on such and such a date I gave that anger to God. It doesn't belong to me any more. If you want to talk about it, you'll have to go to Him. It isn't mine to discuss with you." Turn your back on Satan's lies and allow God's peace to reign in your heart. I always suggest that each one enter the date and commitment in his or her Bible to be a constant reminder.

Recently I was praying about a certain matter and asking God for guidance. He spoke into my heart, "Don't you remember we settled this a long time ago and you wrote it in your Bible?" I did remember, but where? In what Bible? Then it seemed impressed upon me to look in Jeremiah in my Amplified Bible, and sure enough, there it was, dated "June, 1973." O, Lord, how faithful You are!

After you have taken the three basic steps of discovering what you are fighting, of having the roots of your anger exposed, and of making a total commitment of those roots to Jesus Christ, then you are ready to take more specific directions. In the case of "projected and vengeful anger" where the hostility is directed toward a particular person, I suggest four further exercises: Love, pray, forgive and trust that person.

a) *Love that person.* Sincerely pray that God will help you to love that person *as He loves them.* Your human love is not sufficient. You will find yourself saying, "How can I love someone I don't even like?" You can't, but God *can* love them through you if you are willing to expose yourself to His love. How sufficient is God's love? It is

> "...shed abroad (poured out) in our hearts by the Holy Ghost which is given unto us" (Romans 5:5).

Do not be vague in your prayer. Pray definitively. Pray that God's love, compassion and understanding will fill your heart for this one whom you will name in your prayer. Pray in faith knowing that

> "...the effectual fervent prayer of the righteous availeth much" (James 5:16).

As expressed in the Amplified Bible, this is saying that

> "...the earnest (heartfelt, continued) prayer of a righteous man makes tremendous power available — dynamic in its working."

b) *Pray for that person.* Pray specifically for that person in his need, thereby taking the emphasis off your own discomfort and dislike. James asks this pithy question:

> "Doth a fountain send forth at the same place sweet water and bitter?" (James 3:11).

When you are praying for that person and loving him with the love of Jesus, you will find it pretty hard to be despising him at the same time. As you pray, love will supersede anger.

c) *Forgive that person.* I have covered this subject under our discussion on "guilt". However, it is most important to reiterate here. Webster's definition of "forgive" in the *New World Dictionary* is

> "...to give up resentment against or the desire to punish; stop being angry with; to cancel or remit (a debt)."

Unforgiveness and anger seem to be inextricably locked together. Therefore when you truly forgive, anger ceases. You pull out the plug of unforgiveness, and the pot of anger will stop boiling — but not until.

I have told you about Pete and Mary. Although he had repented with bitter tears, it would seem that the hurt was more than she could bear. How could she go on and face the world so bravely? One day she let me in on her little secret. She said this: "If God has forgiven him, who am I that I should not forgive?"

I thought: "What maturity of judgment for one so young!" Because of her attitude, they were able to pick up the pieces of their lives and put them together again. Together they have made their marriage work.

d) *Trust that person again.* There is something else you must do — you must learn to trust that one again. You must give him an opportunity to prove himself again. If God has brought that person to repentance, if He has restored and healed him but *you* do not accept him, you are — in effect — saying you do not trust God nor His purposes.

Bud and Nancy were alcoholics. The story of their lives reads like a cheap novel. Then they met Jesus Christ — what a transformation took place! They got their marriage and their home together again. During the Christmas season about a year later they said, "This is the first Christmas we can remember that we weren't bombed out of our minds."

But there was a nagging problem. Bud had cheated so many times before he came to know the Lord that Nancy couldn't bring herself to trust him. A great strain was put upon their marriage because he was always under suspicion. As we worked it out together, she finally realized that her mistrust of Bud was actually mistrust of the effectiveness of God's work in Bud's life. She was really saying, "Lord, I don't think You did a very good job."

They faced it together, out in the open, and we prayed together. God beautifully restored that trust. It caused Bud to walk tall and square his shoulders to the world. I sat one day and watched Nancy's face wreathed with love and pride as she looked at him.

A teenager said despondently, "My parents don't trust me."
"Why?"
"Well, I did let them down once pretty badly. I was grounded for two weeks. I learned my lesson, but they won't give me another chance. How can I ever prove to them that I wouldn't do it again?"

I talked to the parents, who said, "It's true she did let us down. We can't trust her again." Communication, which had been suspended, was restored to this family when they were willing to talk it out and *trust* again.

* * *

At this point I want to say a word to that person who has wronged another. You have repented with tears of anguish and remorse. You have begged forgiveness from the one you have hurt. But his anger is unabated. What can you do? There are two suggestions I will make here:

Prove your change of heart. In the words of Jesus,

"Bring forth fruit that is consistent with repentance — let your life prove your change of heart" (Matt. 3:8 Amplified).

A remorseful young husband asked me, "How long will it take her to get over the hurt I have caused?" My answer was, "That depends a lot on you and how much you are willing to prove yourself. You will have to walk a straight line. You will have to be gentle and patient, but it will pay off — if you are willing."

Pray till the answer comes. My second suggestion is that you offer earnest, heart-felt prayer for the healing of the one you have hurt *until* the miracle takes place.

* * *

Specific instructions for dealing with explosive and smoldering angers:
1) Medical check-up. 2) Heart searching. 3) Discipline.

Smoldering anger is the more subtle because the person often thinks he is handling it well by keeping it under cover. Yet this same person may be suffering from elusive allergies. He may be ill with various aches and pains. He may be depressed and unhappy. This is why my first suggestion always is to have *a medical check-up* to rule out any underlying illness or disease.

The second suggestion is this: *Search your heart* before God for any root of rebellion or disobedience. This was the Psalmist's prayer:

"Search me, O God, and know my heart; try me and know my thoughts. And see if there be any wicked way in me" (Psalm 139:23-24).

Examine your attitudes, your motives, even your secret thoughts in the light of His Presence. Face up to what He reveals. Don't back away from it and bury it again. Confess it immediately — vocalize it. "Oh, Lord, I didn't realize my attitudes were wrong. My motives were sinful. Forgive me and cleanse me as You have promised in I John 1:9."

The third suggestion is this: You must *exercise self-discipline* in dealing with that old sinful nature of yours. Did you know that one of the greatest battle areas you face is the one within you? No, you did not suddenly become a sinless saint when you became a Christian. Paul makes this very clear in Galatians 5:17, which I now quote fom the New International Version:

"For the sinful nature desires what is contrary to the Spirit, and the Spirit what is contrary to the sinful nature. They are in conflict with each other, so that you do not do what you want."

I read of a man, an elder in his church and respected in the community, who had kept his anger under wraps for fifteen years. Then one day under great stress he blew. He cursed his family in a fit of rage, and then his whole world came tumbling down around him. In despair and remorse, after the turmoil subsided, he concluded, "I am not a Christian — I never was! It is no use now — all is lost."

He did not understand the conflict waging within him, nor the gracious provision God has made for His people. Hear these words of comfort:

> "My dear children, I write this to you so that you will not sin. *But if* anybody does sin, we have One who speaks to the Father in our defense — Jesus Christ, the Righteous One" (I John 2:1 N.I.V.).

What was that dear brother to do? Abandon his faith? Cop out from his Christian life? No! No! All is not lost. The Bible has the answer.

> "Confess...He is faithful and just to forgive...and to cleanse..." (I John 1:9).

Bow at His feet in contrition. "Oh, Lord, I blew it. I thought I had it all under control, but it was too big for me. Forgive me. Help me to get up and go on, and be a stronger man because of this."

Return with me to the scene of the battle exposed in Galatians 5:17, and please note that Paul hems that verse in fore and aft with some very powerful words:

> "So I say, live by the Spirit, and you will not gratify the desires of your sinful nature" (verse 16).

and

> "But if you are led by the Spirit, you are not under the law (of your evil nature)" (verse 18 N.I.V.).

Why? On what grounds?

> "...because through Christ Jesus the law of the Spirit of life set me free from the law of sin and death (which is in my members). For what the law was powerless to do in that it was weakened by our sinful nature, *God did* by sending His own Son in the likeness of sinful man, in order that the righteous requirements of the law might be *fully met in us,* who do not live according to our sinful nature but according to the Spirit" (Rom. 8:2-4 N.I.V.).

Now what does it mean to "walk in the Spirit," to "live in the Spirit," and to be "led by the Spirit"? It simply means that the born-again Christian is "under new management." He no longer obeys the old boss (his sinful appetites and desires), but he heeds only the voice of the Holy Spirit who is the "Spirit of truth." You are not left alone to get by as best you can with your feeble resources. Jesus said:

> "You shall receive *power* after that the Holy Ghost is come upon you; and you shall be witnesses unto Me..." (Acts 1:8).

All the power of Heaven is made available to you through the Holy Spirit in order for you to be an effective witness for Him both in living and in telling. The Greek word for "witness" encompasses all of this. It is "martus" and is translated in other places "martyr". Does that mean we may die for Him? Yes, we may. But it means more too — *power to die to* the old sinful nature and to live unto God. Someone once said to me, "I received the baptism of the Holy Spirit, but I didn't get any great power. My life wasn't any different."

What a tragedy! How foolish it would be to have electrical power wired into your home and still live by the light of a coal oil lamp! You may have beautiful appliances, but they won't work unless you plug them into the electrical outlets. *You* have to use that power — put it to work for you. So it is in the Spirit: You "plug into" the eternal Source of energy through constant daily communion with Him in prayer, praise, worship and the Word. Then you go out and live by that Power. There is no other way.

My friend, we need the Power of His Holy Spirit *actively* at work in our lives in the battle with our old sinful nature. In my Bible I have underlined all the positive things we must do. Among those listed, we are to:

1) "Put off" the old nature.
2) "Mortify" it.
3) "Deprive" it of its power. (Amplified)

But we dare not leave ourselves empty. We must:

1) "Put on" the new man.
2) "Let God's peace rule in our hearts."
3) "Let the word of Christ dwell within us richly in all wisdom." (Col. 3:1-16)

It is a death and a resurrection. We can only truly live in resurrection life when we take our place at the Cross as "crucified with Christ" (Gal. 2:20), acknowledging that we are "dead indeed unto sin and alive unto God...." (Rom. 6:11). What do you do with something that is dead? You bury it. You no longer tend it nor nourish it. It's dead.

Someone has said, "If it's dead, why won't it lie down?"

My answer must be, "Because *you* keep resuscitating it!" For example, when *you* feed the old animosities and angers with suspicion, self-pity or unforgiveness, you simply keep them alive. We must all take our stand that Satan's power over us was broken at the Cross — broken then and for ever.

"Sin shall not have dominion over you" (Rom. 6:14).

The battle was won at Calvary, but if we do not appropriate by faith that wonderful triumph for ourselves, it is like having a million dollars in the bank but living in poverty.

Let me repeat: All the power of Heaven is at your disposal — but *you* must "plug in". I often say, "A light bulb just has to stay plugged in and turned on in order to shine."

Something very beautiful happens when we have "put off" the old self and we are "renewed in the spirit of our minds" by reprogramming our minds with the positive truths of God's Word. We then "put on" the new self which is created to be like God in righteousness and true holiness (Ephesians 4:22-24). Because the Word is effectually at work in us who believe (I Thess. 2:13), it is producing a great change — we are becoming like Jesus in our new nature.

I like to call this process "spiritual photosynthesis". It is comparable to that which takes place in nature when —

"...in the presence of sunlight, the green coloring matter called chlorophyll combines water with carbon dioxide and produces a simple sugar. All life on earth depends upon photosynthesis" (Compton's *Encyclopedia,* page 236).

In our spirits a transformation takes place as the Light of the Lord Jesus shines in our hearts (II Cor. 4:6) and the indwelling Holy Spirit combines our faith with the water of the Word (Eph. 5:26) to produce within us the sweetness and gentleness of the nature of Jesus (II Pet. 1:4).

The following simple diagram may help to make this concept real to you.

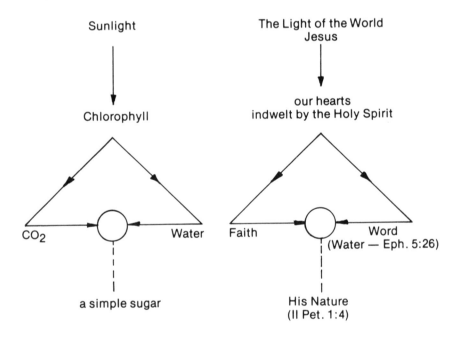

Dr. Francis Schaeffer has said that reading the Bible every day of one's life gives one a different mentality. A Bible "think" is positive, victorious and filled with faith.

I would like to give just another word to those who contend with *explosive anger.* On my pressure cooker there is a gauge. If it registers too high, there is a little petcock I can open to release the excess steam harmlessly. Do you sometimes feel like a pressure cooker? It may be on the job or in the home where little irritations mount up until something threatens to blow. Don't grit your teeth and put the lid on tighter — thereby turning your anger inward and allowing the poison to seep through your whole system. Rather, you must learn to vent that pent-up emotion harmlessly.

Go for a stiff walk. Have a good laugh. Attack a job with gusto. Sing and praise the Lord, offering Him the "fruit of your lips" as in Hebrews 13:15. Your method will depend upon your circumstances. I have used all of these at different times. They are most beneficial. The over-all objective must be to glorify the Lord Jesus. His promise is:

"Call upon Me in the day of trouble; I will deliver thee, and thou shalt glorify me" (Ps. 50:15).

Specific instructions for dealing with inborn anger: 1) Become aware of the hurts which need healing. 2) Establish your identity through the Word of God.

As we come to "inborn anger" and the deep sense of failure and worthlessness which accompanies it, the greatest word that I can give you is this: In Christ there are no hopeless cases. This hope is based on what God says. It is based on the absolutes of God's Word.

We know that everything which has been written in the past has been written for our learning —

"...that we through patience and comfort of the scriptures might have hope" (Rom. 15:4).

Your hope is not fickle or transient — it is "Christ *in you,* the *hope* of glory" (Col. 1:27). The Word of God is our only unfailing absolute. The Psalmist declared:

"Forever, O Lord, Thy Word is settled in heaven" (Ps. 119:89).

I have said all this to you to encourage you to believe and look up — there is hope. Jesus is your Healer. He is the fulfillment of Isaiah's prophecy:

"Himself took our infirmities (or weaknesses), and bare our sicknesses" (Is. 53:4 and Matt. 8:17).

1) *Become aware of the hurts which need healing.* As my first specific direction for you to follow, I say that you must ask the Lord Jesus to walk back with you through the experiences of the past to bring into your conscious awareness the hurts which need His healing touch. You will need help with this, and I would suggest a Spirit-filled counsellor or prayer group who will pray earnestly and carefully with you to bring you to healing. This is part of God's plan for His children.

83

We need one another — no one is an isolated island all by himself. The Scripture makes it very clear that we are:

"...the body of Christ, and members in particular."

There is no division in that body. The members have the same care the one for the other — if one suffers all suffer; if one is honored all rejoice. (Read I Corinthians 12:12-27). We are also told to bear another's burdens (or heavy loads), and in doing so we are fulfilling the law of Christ (Gal. 6:2).

James said we are to confess our faults (or mishaps — those things which have caused us to stumble along life's way) one to another that we may be healed. Then to give some further impetus, he pronounced:

"The effectual fervent prayer of the righteous availeth much" (James 5:16).

It *can* in fact do the job.

My friend, to be a part of the family of God is to be a part of this great provision which He has ordained. Let me give you an illustration of how this works.

I found Elsie crumpled up on her knees with her face buried in her hands and sobbing uncontrollably. In response to my query she said, "It's all so hopeless. Something seems to be driving me. I can't settle down. I flit from one thing to another. I'm angry with myself because I'm so hard on my family — so impatient with them. I'm on the run all the time!"

Elsie is a Christian. She knows Jesus as her Saviour. What she didn't know was that He could walk back with her through her childhood to find the hurts and heal them. We gathered around her to pray. The Holy Spirit showed us a little girl, perhaps five years old, running frantically here and there. She was undisciplined and uncontrolled. No one could hold her nor quieten her. She didn't want to stop long enough to eat or sleep. The path of least resistance seemed to be to let her go her own way. When she was tired enough she would drop in her tracks, and her parents would pick her up and dump her into bed.

As we explained what the Lord was revealing by His Spirit, she began to cry, "That's me! That's me! I see it all now. I see that little girl too, and it is me. It's true!"

Then we prayed that Jesus Himself would step into the picture she was reliving and do what no one else had been able to do — take her into his firm, yet gentle, arms and hold her until all the struggling ceased. Through the eyes of the Spirit, Elsie saw Jesus holding the child that was herself. She saw Him soothing and caressing her, whispering words of comfort into her ear. It had never happened before.

Then a remarkable thing began to take place before our eyes. A quietness and peace like a garment came over Elsie covering her from head to toe. Every twitching nerve was stilled. Her face seemed to shine with a heavenly luminosity. With deep breaths she drank deeply from His well of peace, and with each draft whispered, "Jesus, Jesus. Thank You, Jesus." It was as though she never wanted to leave that hallowed place, and for us it was beautiful to watch. It was for Elsie the beginning of a new life.

I do not wish to present this as a facile thing — it took time. That is why the other members of the body must stand by, continuing to encourage and pray. It is a little like teaching a person to walk all over again.

2) *Establish your identity through the Word of God.* This is my second specific direction for you to follow as you deal with inborn anger. It is essential to your being solidly and permanently grounded in your healing. You must establish — once and for all — your own identity through the Word of God.

Do you know who you are? Let me give you four glorious truths:
a) You are God's child. b) You are His purchased possession. c) You are His workmanship, and d) He will complete His work in you.

a) You are God's child. If you have received Jesus Christ as your Saviour, if you believe that He is the unique Son of God Who died on the Cross for your sins, then according to His Word in John 1:12 you are a child of God by the new birth. Galatians 3:26 states emphatically:

"You are all the children of God by faith in Christ Jesus."

In Chapter Two, remember, I told you about your "birth certificate."

b) You are His "purchased possession". He purchased you at infinite cost — the price was His own precious Blood (Acts 20:28). You are of such inestimable worth to Him that He also put His identifying mark upon you so that all heaven and hell might be called to witness, "This is *My* child, My born again one." We read these words in Ephesians 1:13:

"...after that ye believed, ye were sealed with that Holy Spirit of promise."

The long-awaited Holy Spirit Whom Jesus had promised arrived in His magnificent power on the day of Pentecost as a living proof that Jesus Who died and rose again was now "exalted at the right hand of God" in Heaven (Acts 2:33). This same Holy Spirit has set His seal upon you. You will recognize Him for he comes just as He did "at the beginning" (Acts 11:15). It is as though He is saying: "I have put My Name upon you — it is my 'hold tag' and means that one day I'm coming back to receive you unto Myself, that where I am there you may be also" (John 14:3).

c) You are "His workmanship". You are His handiwork, His special work of art "created in Christ Jesus" for a specific purpose (Ephesians 2:10). In the Old Testament Jeremiah records the object lesson God gave him in the potter's house, and God said:

"As the clay is in the potter's hand, so are you in My hand..."
(Jer. 18:6).

He has taken that lump of clay which is *you,* and He is molding and forming it into a vessel which will be "to the praise of His glory" (Ephesians 1:14). His hands are gentle and firm. Sometimes you start wailing: "Oh, Lord, it hurts too much — I can't stand it." And He says, "Hold steady. You are safe in My hands. There's some grit I have to dig out and some hard spots I have to work over."

Then there comes the time when the vessel has to go through the fire for that special glaze. Again you cry out, "Oh, God! it's too hot. I can't take any more. Let me out." But "walking in the midst of the fire" with you is One "like the Son of God" (Daniel 3:25). He is Jesus Who said, "Lo, I am with you alway (all the days)" (Matt. 28:20). He will not leave you in that fire any longer than is necessary to fulfil His work in your life. And remember this: God does not make failures — He makes winners, only winners.

d) He will finish the work. We are the ones who start jobs and then shove them away somewhere uncompleted. But not so with Jesus. You can

"...be confident of this, that He Who began a good work in you will carry it on to completion until the day of Christ Jesus" (Phil. 1:6 N.I.V.).

One day
"He is going to present you faultless (without a charge against you) before the presence of His glory with exceeding joy" (Jude 24).

That is His ultimate purpose for you. Take heart now,

"...for the sufferings of this present time are not worthy to be compared with the glory which shall be revealed in us" (Rom 8:18).

All that I have given you to establish "who you are" is based on God's inerrant Word. You need never be afraid again. I pray that these words will become your strength and joy — will become a part of the very fabric of your being.

What do we do about "frustrated anger" and all those things which seem to have locked us into a box with walls too high to climb?

Specific directions for dealing with frustrated anger: a) Focus attention off yourself. b) Get the best out of your situation. c) Live one day at a time. d) Greet each new day with a positive attitude. e) Look for something definite to be thankful for. f) Commit every aspect of the situation to the Lord. g) Set right goals.

a) Focus attention off yourself. Direct your attention away from yourself and what seems to be your lot in life. Don't drown in your self pity. Turn your attention to making that one for whom you are caring happier and more contented. Focus on their need for a while. This is how the Bible puts it:

> "In lowliness of mind let each esteem other better than themselves. Look not every man on his own things, but every man also on the things of others" (Phil. 2:3-4).

Margaret was caring for an elderly senile parent and her question was: "How can I do that when the more attention I give Mother, the more demanding she becomes — until she wants an account of my every waking moment?"

I said very gently: "The tables are turned now, and your mother is the little child. Remember that love and discipline go together. You must now be the one who is firm. You must establish discipline with love, just as she once did with you. Basically she is insecure because you are allowing her to ride all over you. Set up firm rules, and stick with them."

b) Get the best out of your situation. Determine how to get the best out of your situation. You can decide whether the problems will be stumbling blocks or stepping stones — whether they will make you better or bitter. Would you stop — right now — and read II Peter 1:5-9? If you have a contemporary translation or paraphrased copy, it will be more clearly understood. I would suggest that you set this out as your pattern of living in your daily situation.

It is God's purpose for you that "you should go and bring forth fruit and that your fruit should remain (be permanent)" (John 15:16). He knows what soil you need, how much rain and sunshine, to bear fruit.

c) Live one day at a time. Focus on today — you have to live only one day at a time. Matthew 6:34 (N.I.V.) says:

> "Do not worry about tomorrow, for tomorrow will worry about itself."

d) Greet each new day with a positive attitude. Instead of "Oh, no, not another day of the same old thing! Why did I ever bother to wake up?", try this tack:

> "This is the day which the Lord hath made; *I will* rejoice and be glad in it" (Psalm 118:24).

Your attitude will not necessarily change the situation, but it will change you. Things look different from above. I have discovered how different the clouds look when I see their topside as I fly in a jet above them.

e) Look for something definite to be thankful for. One person told me she was sure she could find nothing, so I suggested she keep a notebook handy and jot things down over a period of a week. She came back with a big smile and handed me the sheet, saying, "Look, it's full! I had no idea there was so much to thank Him for."

God knows the value of praise in our lives. That's why He exhorts us that "in everything" we are to "give thanks" (I Thess. 5:18).

f) Commit every aspect of the situation to the Lord. Make a total committal. This must be a decisive and definite act of your will. The formula is laid out for you expressly in Psalm 37:5. "Commit thy way unto the Lord." The Hebrew means literally to "roll your way upon the Lord." It's like giving over or dumping the whole thing at His feet. That's just the first part, for it goes on to say: "Trust also in Him." The word trust has great significance because it means to lean upon with complete confidence. If you take one step without the other, you negate the whole thing. You must not only commit your situation but also believe that God is big enough to work it out for your good.

If you do these things, there is a sure and certain result — "He shall bring it to pass," or as the Revised Standard Version gives it: "He will act." When you take your hands off — when you dare to trust Him, you untie His hands (as it were). Then He is able to work out His eternal purposes for you.

Why have you waited so long? Why don't you say right now, "This is it, Lord. I've held it in my hot clammy hands too long. Here it is. I roll it on You now, completely and entirely. Thank You, Lord. My trust is in You, the One Who made this whole universe and commands it by the Word of His power. Hallelujah!" Now isn't that a terrific release?

g) Set right goals. My last instruction or suggestion for handling frustrated anger is to set the right goals. Lay hold of the goals which Paul expressed in Philippians 1:21:

"So *now* also Christ shall be magnified in my body, whether it be by life or by death. For me to live is Christ, and to die is gain."

"Forgetting those things which are behind,...I press toward the mark for the prize of the high calling of God in Christ Jesus" (Phil. 3:13-14).

Specific directions for dealing with peripheral anger

"Peripheral anger" has some directions too. The Christian does not go out and burn down the school because he is angry with the system. Neither does he bury his head in the sand, hoping it will go away. He brings this anger to God and prays:

"Lord, I sense such an urgency to right this wrong. I am Yours, Lord. Show me what to do. Use me as You will to bring Your love and power, Your holiness and mercy, to bear on this situation."

Then do as He tells you, remembering always that His direction is supported by His Word and His character.

Specific directions for dealing with suppressed rebound anger

What about the guilt that results from "suppressed rebound anger"?

Sometimes this is reflected in parents who see the mistakes they made in the raising of their children and now blame themselves for their adolescent and even adult problems. The first thing I would say is this: there is no such thing as a perfect parent. Most parents didn't have prior experience! There is only one thing to do with this. Lay those mistakes at the foot of the Cross where you can find full forgiveness. But you say: "How will that improve their problem? They are stuck with it!"

You must turn the whole mess over to Jesus, for He can make something good come out of it.

Long ago I undertook a knitting project — an Indian sweater for my husband. I was about half way through the back when I realized the pattern was askew and wasn't working correctly. I gave it to Mother, who was known for her knitting skill. She looked it over for a few minutes, then pointed out my mistake about thirty rows back. While I was still gasping, she pulled out the needles from my precious work and ripped back row after row until she came to the error. Then she carefully replaced the needles through each dangling loop and clicked along with her nimble fingers until it was right again.

The Psalmist said:

"Surely the wrath of man shall praise Thee —" (Psalm 76:10).

Come with me to the potter's house in Jeremiah 18:4 and see what God will do. He will:

"...make it again another vessel, as it seemeth good to the potter to make it."

He has put in your hand the most powerful and effective tool. It is prayer in the authority of His Name. Use it daily, conscientiously, with thanksgiving, and

"...if thou canst believe, thou shalt see the glory of God" (John 11:40).

He loves those children even more than you do. Hold them up before Him in the arms of faith, believing Him for their healing and wholeness.

Specific directions for dealing with rebellious anger.
In dealing with "rebellious anger", you must face the problem head-on. The Bible has truly said that

"...the rebellious dwell in a dry land" (Psalm 68:6).

Ken, whose story I told earlier, surely found this to be so. When giving his public testimony, he said:

"It is better to decide one way or the other — to serve God or not to serve Him — than to be floating around in the middle as I was."

If you ever want to know Jesus Christ, you must touch Him for yourself. Jesus is Light. Light is energy. When studying radiant energy I learned that when it touches matter it always makes a change of some kind. You cannot touch Jesus without being changed.

Second-hand faith is totally unsatisfying. A tested, personal faith will cost you something — a total commitment. Only then can you really know its value. I would like to tell you a little incident of our family's personal life to show you how a person prizes most highly that into which he has put something of himself.

It concerns our son who, at sixteen, wanted what every young person dreams of — a car of his own. He got a job pumping gas every day after school and on Saturdays. Finally, he was able to buy a shiny, red Volkswagen Beetle. What a day that was when he brought it home! It was his very own — his pride and joy — purchased with long hours of hard work. One day while he was in the back yard polishing its already dustless exterior, his sister called out the window: "Why don't you put it over your shoulder and burp it?" Doug didn't mind the joking — he was too involved in the reality of what was really his *very own*. And that is the way it is with a personal commitment to Christ — nothing else can truly satisfy.

Now that you have identified and resolved your anger, there are ways for you to remain in victory.

1) *Accept God's surgery as complete.* He doesn't leave any microscopic cells to multiply again. His light, as a laser beam, cuts away all the hurts of the past and heals the wounds so completely that not even a scar remains.

2) *Don't be afraid of the past.* It will not come back to haunt you. Sometimes we have more confidence in our doctor than in our God. If you have had your appendix removed, you don't go poking around to see if it may have grown back again — you know it is gone and you're glad to be rid of it. Do you know why children seldom have post-operative adhesions or what we call "gas pains"? Because they have no fear. They are completely relaxed. Do you recall the little saying I mentioned earlier?

"Fear knocked on the door. Faith opened it and found nothing there."

3) *Forget what is behind.* Now that you are healed, don't look back. There is too much living ahead. There is too much to do. Use Paul's firmness of purpose when he said:

"This one thing I do, forgetting those things which are behind, and reaching unto those things which are before, I press toward the mark for the prize of the high calling of God in Christ Jesus" (Phil. 3:13-14).

4) *Maintain a vital and active daily devotional time.*

5) *Share your joy with someone else.* May I paraphrase Romans 10:9 in this way?

> "*Confess* with your mouth the Lord Jesus and all that He has done for you, and believe in His resurrection power with all your heart, and you shall be made whole."

You must be careful with confession that you do not dig up all the dirt, nor expose another person who may have been involved in that hurt. But share God's great delivering power which brought you out into the light.

Lois discovered the importance of this truth. God had healed her wounds and set her free from the bondage of the past. She settled down into daily living within the family. Then one day she phoned that life seemed to have turned sour.

"How long has it been since you shared your joy with someone else?" I asked.

"I haven't — ever," she answered.

I suggested that she ask the Lord to lead her to another suffering person, and then by the help of the Holy Spirit share with that one His healing power. She did this and phoned again to tell me of the exciting results.

I often say, "You can only keep what you give away," and Jesus said, "Freely you have received, freely give" (Matt. 10:8).

CHAPTER NINE

INROADS OF DEPRESSION

When we talk about depression — which seems to be almost the Number One problem of today's society — we have to consider that which is a normal part of everyone's life and that which becomes a serious affliction. Many people do not want to face the fact that there will be some discomfort and pain in life from which we cannot escape. It is the tensity, the tightness, and duration of depression which determines whether the condition is abnormal. When it interferes with a person's work, his relationship to others and his own self-acceptance, it is serious.

People seem to think that better and more comfortable living can be found through chemistry — thus we have become a pill-oriented society. It was quoted in a Vancouver newspaper of June, 1977, that in Canada an amazing six million tablets of the tranquilizer Valium are prescribed *each week*. Tranquilizers seem to be considered the panacea for just about every symptom of contemporary society — such as loneliness, financial problems, marriage difficulties and even what they call "the empty nest syndrome" (which is the loneliness and depression parents sometimes feel when the children are grown and have flown the nest.)

There is indeed a major problem of depression in our stress-ridden world today, and we must find some answers. During the years of my counselling experience I have uncovered some causes which, I believe, are significant. I do not regard what I have found out as some sort of medical survey as I am not in a position to make that type of judgment, but I will relate them as I found them.

1) *A worn-out motor.* Some people treat their cars better than they do their tired bodies. At least, they put their cars in for a tune-up occasionally, and they do check the oil and battery and fill up with gas. But the old body just has to keep plugging along until eventually something breaks down. God has a reason for giving us one day of rest out of seven. We cannot ignore the principles of His Word without reaping the results in our bodies.

2) *An imbalance in body chemistry or a debilitating illness.* I do not believe the old adage that "ignorance is bliss" — it is plain stupidity and neglect. Thank God for the fine physicians whose knowledge and care are available to us today.

3) *Boredom.* Sometimes this is found in people who have had an active and fulfilling life, and now because of age or health they have had to slow down. They have lost their zest for living and feel that life has simply passed them by. Or it may be that they have never found their place in life, neither in *love* nor in *work* nor in *play.* A person must be fulfilled in all three of these areas or he is sick.

This book and its total concept is for these people. There is a joy in committal. There is a place in Christ for each person, and for those who seek Him He will be found. Don't just sit there. Do something.

4) *Introspection or regret* — a constant looking within in introspection or looking back with regret. I find one of Satan's most effective fiery darts is: "You should have..." or "Why didn't you...?" None of us can go back nor relive our lives again — especially those times and places where we failed and made mistakes — but we can give them to God Who said He would "restore the years" and go on from there. Don't live in the past — the future is as bright as His promises. Don't waste time looking back.

5) *Guilt — the master saboteur.* This is the thing we must deal a death blow to in this chapter. Psychiatrists say that if they could find the answer to guilt, they would have the answer to most of their patients' problems. Dr. Karl Menninger wrote a book entitled *"Whatever Became of Sin?"* He asks the question: "If there is no sin, then why this terrible guilt?"

The answer to this in contemporary society seems to be to call "sin" by the name of "sickness" or "maladjustment" — or in the case of adultery, promiscuity or homosexuality, it is the "new morality" — a way of life. Sometimes it is called a "value system" which is the result of the blending of all the cultures in our global village. Whatever it is called, it does not change God's indictment on the sinfulness of sin.

God's Word, its principles and precepts, His love *and* His judgment — all are universal. They do not vary with the cultural differences. "God so loved the *world*" that He sent His Son to take away "the sins of the *world*" (John 3:16, 1:29). Truth is absolute. It is not determined by the social mores of any people or generation.

Regardless of the cover-up and the rationalizing, *guilt* remains an open festering sore which makes deep inroads into the personality of the whole person. Once again I will draw on my experiences of personal counselling to bring to you the reasons for guilt. The Holy Spirit has brought these to the light — and *these are in the Christian community.*

1) A lack of understanding of the work of the Cross.
2) The haunting fear that maybe someday God will dig up the sins of the past for us to face again.
3) Areas of indecision and non-committal in the life.

A lack of understanding of the work of the cross
May I remind you again of the words of Jesus in Matthew 13:19?

"When anyone heareth the word of the kingdom, *and understandeth it not,* then cometh the wicked one, and catcheth away that which was sown in his heart."

God desires that we understand the Word He has given so that we might

"Always be ready to give a logical defense to anyone who asks us to account for the hope that is in us..." (I Pet. 3:15 Amp.)

We must implant in our intellects, by the enlightenment of the Holy Spirit, the totality of the accomplished work of the Cross. Only in this way will we be able to grasp the magnitude of God's forgiveness through Jesus Christ and thus be freed from the monster called "guilt".

We must understand what actually happened when Jesus died upon that Cross. I have counselled many Christians whose guilt has hung over them like a shroud, and in my deep longing to help them, I asked God to give me a simple, practical, down-to-earth illustration of the power of the Cross.

My thoughts went back to 1942 — the year Lloyd and I were married — when we met and came to love a dear, elderly couple — Sir Ernest and Lady Petter. They had come to Canada to bring a number of children — evacuees — from war-torn England. Sir Ernest had been knighted by the king and was a man of considerable repute. They loved and served the Lord Jesus with all their hearts.

One day Sir Ernest said to me, "Joan, a cataclysmic event is going to happen very soon. Man is going to split the atom, which has always been considered indivisible. I don't know what will happen when they accomplish this, but because of the technological advances of today, they will assuredly split the atom of uranium."

December 2, 1942 is called the birthday of the atomic age — when Dr. Enrico Fermi turned on the first nuclear-energy machine. But the world didn't hear much of this until 1945 — when its first horrendous product, the atomic bomb, unleashed a power of such cataclysmic force that the cities of Hiroshima and Nagasaki in Japan were leveled and World War II was brought to a close.

Now, how does this illustrate the events of the Cross? Atomic power? Yes, and may it grip your heart as it has mine with a clear vision of the infinite power unleashed at the Cross for our salvation. When Jesus Christ the Son of God — ("I and My Father are *one*" (John 10:30), and "He that hath seen Me hath seen the Father" (John 14:9)) — I repeat, when Jesus Christ hung upon that Cross, He not only bore our sins, He actually became our sin.

We read in II Corinthians 5:21:

"For He hath made Him *to be sin* for us, who knew no sin; that we might be made the righteousness of God in Him."

Jesus was even "made a curse for us" (Gal. 3:13), and God cannot look upon sin — sin separates from Him. And in those terrible moments of separation when Jesus cried out from the agony of His soul,

"My God, My God, why hast Thou forsaken Me" (Matt. 27:46)?

God had hidden His face from His Son Who represented the sin of all mankind. It was as though the indivisible Trinity was split, and the force of the power which was unleashed caused the earth to tremble with a great earthquake. The rocks were rent, the sun hid its face, and darkness covered the land from noon until three o'clock in the afternoon. That ornate linen veil of the temple with its heavily embroidered figures of the cherubim, which had separated the Holy Place from the Holy of Holies in the temple, was torn apart from the top to the bottom. At that moment, when God judged sin in Jesus Christ, there was enough power unleashed to forgive every sin that has ever been or will ever be committed by any man, woman or child who will bow in submission at the Cross and receive Jesus as Saviour.

No, God did not just overlook our sin. Be sure that He did not just pat us on the back and say, "There, there, now go your way. I know you didn't mean to sin." Oh, no, it was not that simple. He could not be a just God if He did not exact a penalty, but in His infinite mercy and love He then provided the payment "in full". We must bow at the Cross, believe what Jesus did there on our behalf, and receive Him into our hearts.

Armed with this glorious truth, I now had something tangible, something of substance, to give to those who were so burdened down with guilt. When I first met Anna, her heart was broken. She sobbed uncontrollably as she told me, "I can never be saved. You see, I had an abortion when I was a teenager, and God can never forgive that."

"Can you go back and do anything about it?" I asked her.

"If only I could!" she wept.

"Have you confessed it to the Lord?" I asked.

"Oh, yes, many times!" she replied. "But He cannot forgive abortion."

"Then He cannot forgive anything," I said, "because God does not categorize sin as we do." I showed her Romans 1:29-31, which is God's classification of sin.

He doesn't have little white boxes for those things we call "justifiable sins", nor gray boxes for those things not listed under the "thou shalt not's", nor big black boxes for the heinous sins of murder, sexual vice, theft, etc. He lumps them all under one heading. Gossip, deceit, envy, disobedience, pride — it's all there with murder and every type of wickedness.

Then I told Anna, as I have told you, the illustration of the power unleashed at Calvary. Then we prayed, and the Holy Spirit brought home to her heart, at last, the magnificence of God's forgiveness. Anna raised her arms to Heaven, and her tears of sorrow became tears of joy as she rejoiced and praised the Lord in her new-found freedom. This happened at a retreat, and the next day she came bounding into my room, gave me a quick hug, and danced out of the room singing, "I'm free, I'm free, I'm free!"

Then there was Maureen who had suffered a deep, dark depression for nine long years. Her face seemed to be furrowed with her tears. She was a young woman with three little girls to raise, but she could not cope with the massive problem of life.

"I must have committed some terrible sin, and God is punishing me," she would say to me. So she searched every day with a fine toothed comb, as it were, for the illusive offense. We had spent some time together in a counselling setting, and one day I sent her home to do an exercise in the Word of God. She was to write down all the Scriptures she could find which say, "The Word of God is..." I gave her the first one found in Hebrews 4:12 beginning, "The Word of God is quick, and powerful, and sharper than any two-edged sword...."

Two weeks later Maureen presented me with nine typewritten sheets — she had done her homework well! And the Word had been "effectually at work" (I Thess. 2:13) in her as she studied. We went over each verse again, and then we prayed. She was seated, and as I stood behind her with my hands gently laid upon her shoulders, the Holy Spirit quickened to my mind the words of Hebrew 10:12 — which I repeated:

"But this Man, after he had offered one sacrifice for sins for ever, *sat down* on the right hand of God."

Then followed the words of Hebrews 1:3:

"Who...when He had by Himself purged our sins, *sat down* on the right hand of the Majesty on high."

I stopped for a moment and asked: "Maureen, why do you think Jesus sat down?"

She turned around and looked at me as though this were a completely new thought. Then, her face wreathed in smiles, she said, "Why, I guess it was because He had nothing more to do!" Whatever sin she had ever committed was completely forgiven — she didn't have to go searching any more. The guilt was lifted, rolling off her like a mammoth weight. From that day Maureen began to come out of her depression and to walk into the light of the Lord.

There is a provision for us to deal with guilt, which Jesus Himself instituted in the sacrament of Communion or the Eucharist. He has told us that:

"As *often* as you eat this bread and drink this cup, ye do *shew the Lord's death* till He come" (I Cor. 11:26).

Every time we come to the Communion table we are looking back in acknowledgement to the work of the Cross. But verse twenty-seven tells us that if we eat and drink in an unworthy manner, we eat and drink condemnation to ourselves.

How can this be? We are to examine ourselves before coming to the table of the Lord. I have perceived two ways in which we can come in an "unworthy" manner.

a) *Coming in indifference.* We can come to the table of the Lord as a ritual, indifferently — not "discerning the Lord's body", nor considering His death of much significance. This is because we do not recognize our own sinfulness and our need for continual cleansing. However, the Word of God says:

> "If we say that we have no sin, we deceive ourselves, and the truth is not in us." (I John 1:8).

And again:
> "If we say that we have not sinned, we make Him a liar, and His Word is not in us." (I John 1:10).

b) *Coming in unbelief.* We can come to the table of the Lord in unbelief. This is true when we come confessing our sins and then walk away from the table carrying our guilt. We are, in effect, saying, "Lord, Your death upon the Cross was not adequate to forgive my sins, so I must carry them away with me again." In this way we do not discern His body; we dishonour the work of the Cross and disannul its effectiveness in our lives. We walk away from His table with guilt heaped upon us, and verse thirty tells us:

> "For this cause many are weak and sickly among you, and many sleep."

Guilt, depression and psychosomatic illnesses go hand in hand. We dare not look with indifference upon this provision of God's grace extended so freely to us. And we dare not minimize the work of the Cross lest we eat and drink our own condemnation in an overwhelming sense of guilt.

During a retreat in which I was ministering, God gave me a vivid picture by His Spirit as the people came forward to partake of the Communion. I was standing near the table in prayer, and as each person rose from his knees I saw a pile of dirty, stinking rags forming on the floor. As each one came and left, the pile got a little higher until finally it was very large. I looked at it in wonder. Then a great shovel seemed to come from Heaven and scooped that great pile of rags up in one sweep and threw them into an incinerator. Guilt was lifted from God's people, and we beheld the results in physical healings.

The fear that God will dig up the sins of the past.
The second reason for "guilt" is the haunting fear that God will dig up the sins of the past and that some day we may have to face those sins again. Consequently, there is always a feeling of unrest and insecurity as these things seem to rise from the dark shadows of the past to torment us.

Our confidence is found in the immutability of God's Word — which declares what He has done with our sins. In this regard, I will relate a few of His eternal promises:

"As far as the east is from the west, so far hath He removed our transgressions from us" (Psalm 103:12).

How careful He is with every detail! He specifically stated "as far as the east is from the west," for these are immeasurable distances.

"Blessed are they whose offenses have been forgiven and whose sins have been covered. Blessed is the man whose sin the Lord will *never* count against him" (Rom. 4:7-8 N.I.V.)

"And their sins and iniquities will I remember *no more*" (Heb. 10:17).

And I would like to quote Psalm 130:4 from the Living Bible:

"Lord, if You keep in mind our sins, then who can ever get an answer to his prayers? But You forgive! What an awesome thing this is!"

May I remind you that according to the laws of our land a penalty can never be exacted twice for the same crime. Do you think that God's justice would be any less than this? When you accept Jesus Christ as your Saviour, you endorse the judgment of God on your sin at the Cross. Do you think that His justice is any less than the law of our land? When you know the Scriptures, you can use the "Sword of the Spirit," the "It is written..." to ward off every attack of the evil one when he tries to put guilt upon you.

Areas of indecision and non-committal in the life.

The third reason for "guilt" comes from those areas of indecision and non-committal in our lives. Any areas of rebellion or disobedience in which we refuse to bow to the Lordship of Christ become festering points of guilt. There are those whom I have met who live in a ritual of worship — keeping up a game of pretend for the sake of appearances. They have told me of their nagging guilt.

There are those who refuse to let go of their hatreds and bitternesses. (It is not that they cannot; it is that they *will* not.)

There are those who fill their minds with junk and garbage. They hide these things successfully from their friends and family, yet they live in guilt and fear.

Others are bound by some habit which is destroying their body, but they hang onto it defensively. They wonder why it is so hard to pray, why there is no sweetness of communion, why the guilt.

There are people who constantly feud and cause dissension — they love it, they are "the people that delight in war" (Psalm 68:30) yet, underneath, their guilt irks them on until they can hardly live with themselves.

I would like to tell a little story which I believe speaks volumes. There was a little girl who was allergic to cats. One day she arrived home from school sniffing, sneezing and wheezing. Her mother cried out, "What happened to you?" Then she noticed that the child had her coat held tightly at her neck. "What are you holding?" the mother asked. And at that moment she heard a muffled "Meow!" The little girl opened her coat, and there nestled against her chest was a dear little kitten. Mother said, "Honey, I'm sorry, but you cannot possibly keep it. Look! You can hardly breathe now. You must immediately take it back where it came from." The child walked down the street weeping and returned it to her little friend a few houses away. The next morning, however, when Mother was preparing breakfast, she heard a sound on the back porch — "Meow!" She opened the door, and there was the kitten lapping at a saucer of milk which the little girl had placed there — "just in case..."

I have discovered many people who keep their "saucer of milk" handy — just in case. There was Alice, who asked for help with her drinking problem. She told me that she sincerely wanted to be free, but we weren't progressing at all. She continually fell back. One day she told me that she kept a pop bottle of liquor in her car — just in case.

Then there was Trudy, who suffered a lengthy depression and seemed to live under a cloud. While I was praying about her one day, the Holy Spirit seemed to impress me to ask her if she had ever had anything to do with fortune telling. She was a Christian, and I asked the Lord to give me great wisdom when I asked her this.

"Yes, I used to read people's cards," was her rather reticent response, "but that was many years ago."

I waited for a few moments. Then I asked again, "When did you do it last?"

"About a month ago," she replied, her answer even more hesitant. "You see, I still have the cards, and a friend came and begged me to read them for her. I did it, and immediately I knew it was wrong."

I read to Trudy from Deuteronomy 18:10-12 — God's warning about fortune telling and such occult practices. I asked her if she was willing to confess her sin, renounce all such things, and burn the cards. In her intense longing to be well, she willingly obeyed. From that moment she began to come into freedom and victory. Her depression lifted and she entered a most fruitful life of helping others to find wholeness in Jesus Christ.

I wonder if you have a "saucer of milk" which is loading you down with guilt and robbing you of an effective Christian witness? Here are some very forceful words from Romans 6:16 in the Amplified version of the Bible:

"Do you know that if you continually surrender yourselves to any one to do his will, you are the slaves of him whom you obey?"

Will you consider now the question, "Is that saucer of milk really worth it?" You can be lifted from your guilt and its consequences, you can walk into the Light and be free if you will bow at the Cross and make Jesus the

Lord of your whole life. I pray that you will do this right now, as I help you with this prayer:

"Lord Jesus, I have held onto a saucer of milk." (You must name it — confess it with your mouth.)

"I know that it has enslaved me, and I want to be free. I want to live completely for You. I give this thing to You now, and with Your help I will not take it back. Give me the strength I need to overcome. I confess You now as my Lord, and I rejoice in Your power to deliver me and to set me free. Thank You, Jesus. I ask this in Your dear Name, Amen."

CHAPTER TEN

HEALING IN THE FAMILY — I

It is time for us to deal with the horizontal relationships of our lives. Each one of us has a deep responsibility in the family, whether it be to one another in the home or to the larger family of God. Jesus' commission is: "As the Father hath sent Me, so send I you" (John 20:21). We have a job to do. His promise is:

"He that believeth on Me, the works that I do shall he do also; and *greater* than these shall he do; *because* I go unto My Father" (John 14:12).

What works did Jesus do? He stood in the synagogue one day and read, as recorded in Luke 4:18,

"The Spirit of the Lord is upon Me, for He hath anointed Me to preach the gospel to the poor; He hath sent Me to heal the broken-hearted, to preach deliverance to the captives, and recovering of sight to the blind, to set at liberty them that are bruised."

He didn't go back to Heaven and leave humanity in its helpless condition to get along as best it could. He provided for a continuance of His work. He chose us who believe to be "workers together with God" to bring healing and wholeness in His Name. The exhortation of Scripture is clear:

"Bear ye one another's burdens, and so fulfil the law of Christ" (Gal. 6:2).

Burdens are those things which weigh people down and cause them to stumble. When we share these heavy weights we are fulfilling "the law of Christ" which is love. Romans 13:10 says:

"Love worketh no ill to his neighbour: therefore love is the fulfilling of the law."

The instructions of Jesus are explicit, and they are founded on love.

This responsibility of ministry within the family — whether the home family or the church family — is not optional. It is first, the obedient response of love and second, the proof of discipleship.

103

We read in John 21:15-17 that Jesus asked three times, "Peter, do you love Me?" Each time Peter answered, "Yes, Lord, You know that I love You." Jesus replied, "Feed My (little) lambs," and then He repeated twice, "Feed My sheep." This is the responsibility of love. The word "feed" which Jesus used here means literally "to tend as a shepherd, to nourish and care for." The shepherd is willing to go out into the storm for the one lost sheep.

Love is the proof of discipleship. Jesus said, "By this shall all men know that ye are My disciples, if ye have love one to another" (John 13:35). God has set His people in His family. We are "one body in Christ, and every one members one of another." (Romans 12:5).

"And whether one member suffer, all the members suffer with it; or one member be honoured, all the members rejoice with it" (I Cor. 12:26).

I remember, rather poignantly, the time I caught the tip of my little finger in the car door. Now I didn't scold nor berate that offending member. I didn't tell it how stupid it was to get in the way. Instead, I cuddled it and soothed it. I held it tightly, and I cried a little too — you see, it was part of my body. In fact, I ached all over for my poor little finger! And this is how it is in the body of Christ.

The supreme catalyst is love. But we can never know real love until we touch Jesus Who is the essence of pure love. *He is love.* Our human love is selfish. It says, "What am *I* going to get out of it?" or "What's in it for *me*?" Human love demands an acceptable performance, saying in effect, "If you please me, I will love you," but the love of Jesus says, "I will love you regardless."

In order to bring healing to the family, we must first of all be sure that we are building on the right foundation. The Bible says, "Other foundation can no man lay than that is laid, which is Jesus Christ" (I Corinthians 3:11), and I Peter 2:6 reminds us that He is "the chief corner stone, elect, precious." And the home, the family, the person that builds on that Foundation "shall not be confounded."

Why do I know that He is the only solid foundation on which to build? Because everything around us is unstable, shifting, uncertain — only He remains unchanged — and changeless, "in whom is no variableness, neither shadow of turning" (James 1:17).

There is no other security except in Him. I have seen homes and marriages fall apart when people walk away from God, forsaking "the old landmark" which their parents have set for something that is not proven. (See Proverbs 23:10).

Some young people have said to me, "Mrs. James, my parents don't believe in anything," and because of this, they have nothing secure upon which to build their lives.

There is always hope in God, and any young person in this insecure position can "raise up the foundations of many generations" (Isaiah 58:12) as he builds his life on Jesus Christ. We can all start building on this

Foundation a firm superstructure — represented in this study by the four C's: Communication, Concern, Commendation and Compassion.

Communication

Defined by Webster, communication means "an exchange of information" or "a close and sympathetic relationship." It is a two-way street, a giving and receiving between two people. It may not necessarily always be verbal — it may be the squeeze of a hand or a mutual understanding in the meeting of the eyes.

How communication is given and how it is received is most significant. The type of communication which restores and builds is not an interchange of verbal or physical abuse, neither is it a look of daggers across the room, nor a menacing kick under the table.

What communication is not: I will try to illustrate graphically what I do not mean by communication. *Communication is not static.*

Static

In this instance both are giving at the same time and the end result is confusion and static.

In an earlier chapter I mentioned George and Alice, the young couple who came for marriage counselling. Previously they had attended a group therapy session in which a number of couples were involved. They sat in a circle and verbally lashed out at one another with all the hate they could muster up. It was a shattering experience for both of them.

"How do you feel now?" I asked.

"Terrible!" they both responded at once. (It was the one thing they agreed upon!)

"We'll never get our marriage together now," Alice said in dejection and hopelessness. "We have hurt one another beyond repair."

Thank God that Jesus is the One Who puts marriages together again, and He did this for George and Alice. Today they are walking hand in hand, and they face the future with confidence and assurance.

Communication is not what I call "the marital sound barrier."

Silence

A   B

The only thing that seems to break through the marital sound barrier is a "sonic boom" when one or the other finally explodes in anger. One lady told me, "we don't even talk at the meal table. If my husband wants the salt shaker and it's on the other side of the table, he will walk around the table to get it rather than speak." Then she added, "I cannot stand this unutterable silence."

Communication is not something I call subjugation. I illustrate it like this:

Subjugation

One person does all the talking, all the deciding, and makes all the moves. The other retreats behind a wall of silence, timidity, a martyr complex or fear. This is a distortion of the Biblical concept of submission as given in the *total context* of Ephesians 5:21-25. To keep the teaching in correct proportion, notice that the first word given speaks of *mutual* submission.

"Submitting yourselves one to another in the fear of God" (Eph. 5:21).

This type of communication which I call "subjugation" can happen from either side of the marital team.

A woman who was very unhappy in her marriage told me at great length that her husband was a Mr. Milquetoast. She complained in no uncertain terms that he did not take his place in the home as the "head". He would never make a decision, he would not correct the children, he simply was a nonentity. It didn't take me long to figure out why. What chance did he have with this dominant woman? He had simply given up and retreated behind his newspaper.

When I pointed this out to her, she was shocked and not a little mortified. "What shall I do?" she asked. "Is it too late?" I told her it was never too late to bring Jesus into the picture. I suggested first of all that she confess to Him her foolishness, selfishness and disobedience.

With tears of repentance, she did confess her sins. Then I asked her if she and her husband could read the Bible together. (It is amazing — but some couples, even though they are both Christians, cannot.) "Oh, yes, we can read the Bible together," she said.

"Then you get your Bible and open it to Ephesians 5 and I Peter 3," I continued. "Sit down beside him (and be sure you pick a convenient time.) Say, 'Honey,' — or whatever you call him — 'I want to read to you about God's order in the home. I want to tell you how sorry I am that I have been so dominant. I haven't given you a chance. I have overruled and out-ruled you. Please forgive me. I love you, I respect you. I want you to have your rightful place in our home, and I will pray for you and support you from now on in every way. I have confessed my neglect and my overbearing manner to the Lord, and I have asked Him to change me and to make me the kind of wife and mother He wants me to be'."

Do you know that about two weeks later I heard that things were entirely different in this home, and God was bringing into the family a new and beautiful dimension of living. I heard a little saying a long time ago that I think is most applicable. It works both ways, but as I am a woman I will direct it to the wives. Here it is:

> "The things you criticize your husband for may be the things which kept him from getting a better wife."

Communication is not manipulation. This one-sided type of communication described in "subjugation" can also become manipulation:

Manipulation

I have talked to distraught parents who have told me that their teenager is threatening to move out if they do not let down on some of their restrictions. That son or daughter is rebelling frantically against parental authority, saying that Mom and Dad are archaic, have no understanding of young people today and "Don't they realize that everyone else has free reins?"And so the parents are manipulated into a corner while son or daughter pulls the strings. This type of situation is not unusual. We face it almost every day.

The first thing I must say to parents is that you must not renege when it comes to the principles of God's Word. But, if what you are seeking to enforce is merely tradition, then you had better take a second look. Whatever you do, be honest. And keep those communication lines open. I have talked to many young people, and although they rebel and kick like young steers, they *do not* want their parents to let down their proven standards. This is their security and they know it.

While counselling in a detention home, I was told by one young person, "I only wish my parents would have said 'No!', but every time I asked them what I should do, they would say, 'It's your life. Do as you please'." In despair this young person continued, "Mrs. James, I didn't know what decision to make myself!"

Young people need the security of your maturity. I had taught a teenage class for many years and began to wonder if my teaching was really relevant. When I mentioned this one time, their answer was: "Oh, yes! We need to learn by *your* experience."

What communication is: Now let us look at some positive things about communication. a) There must be a willingness to *listen with our hearts.* When God appeared to Solomon in a dream and said, "Ask what I shall give you," Solomon replied:

> "Give Your servant an understanding mind and *a hearing heart* to judge Your people" (I Kings 3:9 Amp.).

Too often we hear only with our ears what the other is trying to say, and it's nothing but a cacophony of meaningless sound. Unless we listen with our hearts, we will not really hear the longing or the hurt which is seeking for expression and help. How many lengthy ramblings would be shortened if we would only involve our hearts in our listening rather than waiting impatiently for the other person to finish talking so we can get in our two cents' worth!

b) In true communication there must be a willingness to *respond honestly, gently and objectively.* I am a sensitive person and until I learned how to channel this sensitivity by the Holy Spirit, it often was my undoing. One time, during a family tiff, my husband said to me, "You are far too sensitive." Now my response was not exactly any of these three things. With hands on hips, and eyes flashing, I let it be known in no uncertain tones: "I — am — not — sensitive!" Well, I proved one thing: I am sensitive.

c) In real communication we must be willing to *listen with a non-critical, non-judgmental heart.*

A friend of mine was very upset one day. She told me that her son had come home from school the previous evening and had told her that the kids in his class were smoking marijuana. I asked her, "What did you say?"

"Oh," she said, "I just blew! I was furious."

"What did he do?" I asked.

"He walked out of the house and slammed the door," she replied. What a tragedy! Not only the door of the house but the door of communication was slammed shut.

"Oh, my dear," I said, "why didn't you say, 'Son, sit down and tell me all about this stuff — this marijuana'?"

We must keep the communication lines open at all costs. I have found through counselling that if I sit in criticism, shock, or judgment, that person retreats and there is no way I can reach in to help.

d) In positive communication there must be a willingness to *be the one to break the deadlock.* If one clams up or goes into a shell, will you be quick to break the deadlock? Remember, it takes two to communicate. Don't be afraid to say, "I'm sorry. I was wrong," and to say it freely, *ungrudgingly.* After all, does it really matter who was right? Is it really worth making an international incident out of it? In our family it seems I am the one who makes most of the goofs, so usually I'm the one who has to apologize. One day I said to my husband, "It must be wonderful to always be right!" His quick retort was, "It is. Why don't you try it some time?" We have found that a sense of humour goes a long way in breaking deadlocks. Laugh a lot. Laugh *with* one another, and laugh *at* yourself.

Here are a few other things that help in breaking deadlocks. A little gift or a thoughtful act. Bake his favourite pie. Bring her home a rosebud. Cultivate an understanding spirit of gentleness.

One man decided to break the sound barrier by taking his wife out to dinner in a very intimate restaurant where tables were set for two and couples could sit quietly together in a lovely relationship. As they sat in silence, he noticed that they were surrounded by young couples who, with hands clasped across the table, were looking into one another's eyes and talking animatedly. To him, their own silence seemed out of place in such a setting. Reaching out, he took her hand, looked intently into her face and said warmly, "Mary had a little lamb; its fleece was white as snow..." She laughed spontaneously, and the ice was broken.

e) In positive communication there must be a willingness to *let the past lie buried*. A little bride phoned me in tears. "I don't know what to do," she said. "Jack wants me to tell him all that I ever did in my life. Mrs. James, I can't tell him all that stuff. Jesus has forgiven me. Why do I have to drag it out now?"

"Put Jack on the phone," I said. When he came on the line, he said he thought it was only right that she should tell him everything. I told him that if he wanted to destroy his marriage at its very beginning he was going about it the right way. "You have absolutely no right to be digging around in God's garbage dump," I said. "That is none of your business. What God has forgiven is buried, covered, and forgotten."

f) In maintaining good communication there must be a willingness to *recognize a problem* — and that problem could be *you*. Often, when dealing with family relationships, I have found that each sits tight in his own position thinking that the other one is totally at fault.

When Sally and Jack came for counselling, they had been separated for a while and were scarcely on speaking terms. Each had retreated into the "poor me" attitude. Because I had insisted upon it, they arrived at my door together. But neither acknowledged the other and both were wrapped in a cloak of self pity.

Sally's complaint was that whenever she tried to talk about their problems he went out the door and she wouldn't see him for hours. Jack's lament was that as soon as he tried to reason with her she burst into tears — and he couldn't stand tears. I told them that I would not allow them to lash out at one another, that I was going to treat them like mature people because marriage is not for the immature.

They had an opportunity to air their views quietly and reasonably. As they began to see one another's problems before their own, a new understanding was born. Finally after prayer and positive direction from

God's Word, they went home together hand in hand.

Marie was the teenager I have previously mentioned who told me that her parents neither understood nor trusted her. She admitted that she had let them down pretty badly in a certain instance but that she had made it right. Still there was no communication. It seemed to be a closed subject. She said, "How can I ever prove myself if they won't trust me again?" When I talked to the parents, they said, "It's true. We don't trust her. She broke our confidence, and that's that."

They agreed to come together for help, to try to restore the communication lines again. I asked each one to express aloud what they had told me privately.

When Marie was willing to listen to what her parents had to say, her reaction was: "But Mom and Dad! I never realized you felt this way!"

"We know," they said, "because every time we tried to talk with you, you ran into your room, shut the door, and turned your stereo on full blast."

When the parents were willing to listen to Marie as she told her side, they said, "But, Honey! We never knew you felt this way!"

"Every time I tried to talk to you," she replied, "you got so upset and uptight I just couldn't get through to you, so I just gave up."

As they talked it out honestly, gently and objectively, they were able to extend their hearts to one another again in love and forgiveness.

In both of these situations there was a willingness from all concerned to seek additional help. No one said, "You can go for counselling. The problem is yours, not mine." Each was willing to become involved, and therefore solutions were found.

g) In marriage there must be a willingness to *be both a lover and a friend.* Some are great friends, going places and doing things together but the intimacy of love is absent. For others everything happens in the bedroom, and afterwards they are like two strangers, each going separate ways. Successful marriages cannot be built without a blending of the two.

In pre-marital counselling I have found it necessary to teach young people that they cannot build a marriage on sex alone. They must find areas of mutual enjoyment and participation such as sports, hobbies, music or books — explore the possibilities. Patterns of good communication in the areas of finances, having children, commitment to a church, work and vocations should begin before marriage. Then after the wedding bells and all the excitement has ended, you settle down to make these patterns work. Someone has said:

"Marriages may be made in Heaven, but the maintenance department is down here."

In marriage counselling we find one of the areas of greatest stress is the sexual. There are so many hurts, hang-ups and preconceived notions surrounding this vital part of the marriage. I do not intend to discuss this at length. There are many good Christian books on the subject. However, I will deal in the area of healing.

Some people enter marriage with the deep hurts and abuses of childhood unresolved. Carried over into the adult life, these hurts cause intense frustration. Some have grown up thinking that sex is dirty and evil. For such people sex in marriage doesn't suddenly become an act of purity. I will give you two illustrations of the marvellous healing power of the Lord Jesus.

The marriage of one young couple was being torn apart because he was a homosexual. Recognizing his desperate need, he cast himself upon the Lord. As we prayed, the Holy Spirit walked back into his childhood and brought to his memory some very painful experiences. He had been rejected by his father — a stern disciplinarian who had no time for affection or warmth. He wept as he recalled, "I longed to have my Dad just put his arm around me, or show me some love. But he never did. I was starved for love. Then when I was a teenager, a man came along who showed me the affection I longed for. But he introduced me to homosexual practices, and before I realized what was happening, I was involved."

This young man hated the whole thing, but he was caught in a web from which he wasn't able to escape. We asked the Lord Jesus to heal the rejected, hurting boy and to put His pure arms of love around him. The healing power of Jesus Christ began to remold that young man's life and brought him complete deliverance. One day his little wife said to me, "I really am his wife at last. I'm so glad we didn't give up."

Then there was Patty who had learned from childhood that sex was dirty. She remembered a frightening thing that happened to her in school as a little girl. She couldn't talk to her mother about it because sex was a no-no subject in their house. When she was married, she carried all this with her and the frustration was unbearable. Jesus the Healer walked into her life too and healed all those hurts and memories. Then we re-programmed her thinking with the Word of God. We showed her that "sex" was God's idea, that He meant it to be a warm and beautiful thing between husband and wife. But the devil had distorted it and made it ugly. We read the Scripture in Genesis 2:24 — which was also quoted by Jesus in Matthew 19:5:

"For this cause shall a man leave father and mother, and shall cleave to his wife; and they twain shall be one flesh."

God even likens the love between husband and wife to that between Christ and His church. We find this beautiful comparison in Ephesians 5:23-33. I would suggest that you meditate upon this portion of the Word. Patty received her healing from Jesus, and her marriage became all that she could wish it to be.

h) In marriage there must be a willingness to *pray together*. Parents, teach your children the simplicity of prayer from their earliest childhood. Don't make a heavy out of it. Young people have said to me, "Our family altar is an endurance contest. Dad has to pray around the world, and then some!" How much better a simple prayer committing one another to the

Lord before we separate for our various activities. And a short Scripture to carry in our minds.

Sally and Jack, whom I have already mentioned, had started off their marriage with great expectations. Every morning before going to their separate jobs they would read a chapter and spend about half an hour in prayer. But the trouble was that sometimes they were a little late getting up, and then there was this hassle about devotions. Jack insisted that they must do their regular time, and sometimes Sally was late for work. Soon resentment and irritation clouded their parting each morning. Then they decided to give up their devotions altogether — they figured it just wasn't going to work. Of course it wasn't long before their marriage was in trouble, and they separated.

When Sally and Jack got their marriage together again, I made a suggestion (which has worked in our marriage for thirty-five years): "Don't make a heavy out of your morning devotions. Read a few verses of the Word of God together (we like the Daily Light) then in a simple prayer commit one another to the Lord for the day and part friends. You will find this won't bog down. It wears well. I know."

*   *   *

In bringing this discussion of communication to a close, may I give a word to *sons and daughters* of any age? Don't shut your parents out. It is equally your responsibility to keep the communication lines open. Perhaps you should try walking in their shoes for a while. You see, it's not easy raising you and trying to give you the best life with possibly limited finances. But your parents are doing their best. So please don't blame them. Just love them. And if you feel they failed you, forgive them. There is no such thing as a perfect parent, and none of them had any prior experience. Pray for them. Whatever they may have done to hurt you, they are still your parents, and God's Word still holds — "Honour your father and your mother." This injunction is repeated seven times in the New Testament.

CHAPTER ELEVEN

HEALING IN THE FAMILY II

We have suggested four C's necessary in the healing of family relationships — Communication, Concern, Commendation and Compassion. In the last chapter we dealt at length with communication. And now the next building block is concern.

Concern is the ability to understand another's need above our own. The main thrust of this book has been healing for the whole person — spiritually, emotionally, intellectually, physically and socially. Every human being has basic needs in every one of these areas. Let us look at them again for a moment.

Spiritually — the desire to worship, to touch something beyond oneself.

Emotionally — the need to love and be loved, to experience joy *and* sorrow, for sunshine and rain are equally necessary.

Intellectually — the craving for knowledge, regardless of how basic it may be.

Physically — the common need for food and shelter — and for the touch of a human hand.

Psychologists tell us that an infant kept in an incubator too long without being held in the warmth and security of human arms will suffer irreparable emotional damage.

Socially — we need one another. We are social beings.

I once heard the story of a little boy who was afraid of thunder. He slept in an upstairs bedroom, and one particularly stormy night it seemed to him that the thunder was going to come right through the roof. After his mother had prayed with him and tucked him in for the night, she said, "Now, Johnny, it's all right. You don't need to be afraid. Jesus is with you." The scared little boy looked up wistfully and said, "I know, Mommy, but I need someone with skin on." Yes, it is true, we do need one another. No one is an isolated entity.

The person who is hurting or deprived in any one of these areas will be affected in his outlook, his attitudes and his motivation. That one who is so difficult to live with or who lashes out in spite and hatred may be suffering hurts he is not aware of or has covered up in fear because he cannot cope with them objectively.

An understanding of this in *our* hearts will manifest itself in genuine concern. Rather than giving such a hurting person the brush-off, we will pray for him in depth and sincerity.

Have you ever wondered how Peter could have denied the Lord in His hour of trial — even cursing and swearing that he did not know the Man? Perhaps we have judged Peter too severely. Let us look back to the Garden of Gethsemane where it all began.

It was night when Judas came with a "great band of men and officers... with lanterns and torches and swords." They laid hands on Jesus and arrested Him. Of all the disciples Peter alone jumped to His defense. Whipping out his sword, he cut off the ear of the high priest's servant. Undoubtedly he was rather proud of this display of courage. He may have looked back at the others as if to say, "What's the matter with you guys? Am I the only one willing to defend our Lord?"

When he turned back to Jesus, expecting words of commendation, he received a rebuff instead. Then to his amazement and chagrin, he saw Jesus pick up the severed ear, replace it and heal the servant with a touch. What a blow to Peter's pride! What a let-down! Any one of us would have retreated to lick our wounds.

All the disciples fled in terror, but as the retinue of soldiers took Jesus away, Peter and another disciple did follow — even though "afar off". Because the other disciple was known to the high priest, he got inside. Tenacious Peter refused to budge, and he hung around the door until a maid let him in. It was cold. He huddled near the fire, apparently unnoticed by the temple servants and officers. He had time now to mull over his rejection. The hurt feelings grew so big that he was ready to deny any association with Jesus at all. Then, challenged by the little maid, he just blew up. But Jesus knew all that pent-up emotion. He understood, and in the midst of all the mockery He was receiving, He "turned and looked upon Peter."

The Bible says that "Peter went out and wept bitterly". He wept tears of remorse for his denial and failure. But I believe something happened when Jesus looked at Peter. When their eyes met, Peter found understanding, forgiveness, healing.

Peter had been deeply hurt, but Jesus was making a man out of Peter. He looked ahead and saw Peter as he would be on the day of Pentecost — a man charged with the power of the Holy Spirit.

Concern is the ability to see another person's identity crisis — his need to accept himself. How can we love our neighbour if we do not love ourselves? If we have no respect for our own worth, we will have none for that of our neighbour. Lack of self-worth causes people to destroy one another. Human life becomes of little value. I have talked to those who have buried themselves in alcohol, drugs and sex who have told me, "Well, my life isn't worth anything anyhow."

I have discovered some reasons for this terrible sense of worthlessness: 1) Put down, 2) Impossible goals, 3) Identity crisis, 4) Accusation, 5) Rootlessness.

1) There are those who have always been put down by parents, family or school teachers. They are never commended, never challenged to rise to their potential. They have come to accept failure as their norm.

2) There are those for whom parents or peers have set impossible goals — often because of social prestige. Pushed beyond their abilities, they fail. I have talked to young people who have copped out on drugs because of this kind of pressure.

3) There are those who never accept their own identity. They continually strive to emulate someone else. They may have become the successor to someone whom they greatly admire — they seek not only to fill the position but *to be* that person. This never works. It simply becomes a hopeless charade. We must be ourselves. I discovered this in my own experience.

Once when I was one of the speakers at a retreat, the other speaker just completely overwhelmed me. She was everything I would like to have been — a great personality, a superb orator, very sure of herself. I said, "Lord, please let me go home. I just don't think I can compete with that." I walked through the retreat grounds wrestling with this thing until He spoke to my heart. This is what He said. "I haven't asked you to be this other speaker. I have only asked you to be yourself. Neither have I asked her to be you. She too must be herself. And there is no competition." My heart welled up in gratitude. There was no further hassle. Jesus accepted me as I was — then so must I.

4) There are those who listen to this accusing voice of Satan. He is "the accuser of the brethren" (Revelation 12:10). Such a voice is never from God. We have power in the Name of Jesus to be free from that torment.

5) There are those who have no roots of natural birth, and they feel they have no real identity. Not long ago I read in a Vancouver newspaper the words of a prominent U.S. criminologist, who said:

"Many people may have suffered irreversible personality damage because of a traumatic past. No prison, no probation department, no psychiatrist can provide a new childhood, and for some, anything but a new childhood is too little too late."

As I read the apparent hopelessness of this statement, my heart cried out, "But I know Someone Who can do better than that. He can give us a new birth, and a whole new clean sheet on which to write the story of our lives."

It is true. Jesus can give us a new birth. He can give us a reason for living. He can heal and blot out the trauma of the past. He can give us the security of belonging. The answer to all the identity crises is found in Jesus Christ and in Him alone.

Just recently a young man stood before me with tears running down his face. After listening to an inner healing seminar, he said, "At last I know who I am. At last I belong."

The understanding of these things gives us a concern for the other person's need. And concern means forgetting ourselves in order to bring him to healing and wholeness.

Concern also means a respect for each other's individual personalities. We cannot possess one another — whether a child, a spouse or a friend.

If we clutch our loved ones tightly to ourselves or try to squeeze them into our mold, we lose them. We must hold them with open hand. Then they know that the relationship is one of love — not of coercion.

How often those who were held in a tight, suffocating relationship have said to me, "I have no room for expression. I feel closed in. Something inside me is crying out, 'Let me be me'!" Each person needs time to be alone, to think, to pray — to know his privacy will not be infringed upon. When there is trustful, loving concern, we do not put one another in a box. Neither do we take advantage of the other's trust by selfishly doing our own thing at the other's expense.

A word to parents — We parents must learn to hold our children in an open hand — loosely. They are only loaned to us. Sometimes young people feel smothered by their parents' concern. They say to me, "My folks don't trust me at all. If I decide to shut my bedroom door for a little while, in no time flat Mom comes barging in to see what I'm doing. For goodness' sake, what does she think anyway?" I'm just telling you what the kids have said to me. Please, Mom, wouldn't it be better to knock on the door and say, "Is it okay if I come in?" Grant them the courtesy you expect of them when you are in your room.

Remember there must come a time when we are willing for the umbilical cord of parental attachments to be cut. If we hold our children too tightly, we will both be hurt in their struggle to escape. We must let our children grow up; we must trust that what we have taught them throughout childhood will stand them in good stead now that they are trying their wings. We could learn from the birds who push the fledglings out of the nest — then hover nearby to protect their little ones.

I remember the icy feeling in my heart when my daughter left home for the first time to go to college a thousand miles away. She was eighteen. I was so afraid that I hadn't taught her well — that I hadn't prepared her for life's dangers and hurts. Then I remembered that the Lord would be there with her, He is always faithful and I could confidently place her in His Hands.

Mother, if your daughter decides that she wants to be her own woman with her own little apartment, don't take it as a personal affront. Don't be afraid. God loves her more than you do, and it is all a part of growing up. Do you know what some girls have told me? They have said, "My Mom and I are such good friends — closer now than we ever were before!"

A word to those married to unbelievers. Your husband is not a Christian? Your wife does not yet know the Lord? And you stand alone in your faith. Many times you feel like throwing in the sponge and giving up. You say it would be easier to leave your mate than to live with him?

Paul gives some instructions regarding this very matter in I Corinthians 7:12-14. He tells us that if any brother has a wife who does not believe in Christ, he is not to leave her if she consents to live with him. If any woman has an unbelieving husband, she is not to leave him if he consents to live with her. Paul makes it clear that he is speaking — not the Lord, for Jesus did not discuss this. Paul's basis for his instruction is found in verse fourteen. There he says that the unbelieving husband is sanctified by the believing wife — and vice versa. So in view of this, *if it is at all possible,* remain with your mate. Let the love and life of Jesus Christ flow through you to him. You are his link to Heaven. Be encouraged by this word from I Peter 3:1 which says you may win that unbelieving spouse by your godly and loving life — even "without a word." We have heard the testimony of many who have come to the Lord in this way. So take heart — your God is faithful.

But if you find that for health reasons, or physical safety, you have to leave — then don't beat yourself with it. Don't condemn yourself. Don't live in guilt. Jesus understands — He will not accuse. He died for you (Romans 8:33-34). But do not leave with bitterness or unforgiveness in your heart. Keep on praying for that one whom Jesus loves and died for too. Pray with faith in your heart.

A word now to the unmarried, the widowed, the divorced or separated. The Bible says:

> "God places the solitary in families and gives the desolate a home in which to dwell" (Psalm 68:6).

You have a place in the family of God, and no one should ever be lonely in His family. Do not look upon yourself as an oddball, a misfit, a reject. You are none of these. God has a place and a beautiful plan for your life. He hasn't finished with you yet. Fulfilment is not found in being married or unmarried. It is found in commitment to Jesus Christ. So get with it. Forget your own loneliness and set out to fill someone else's loneliness. Jesus came the first time "not to be ministered unto, but to minister" (Mark 10:45), and as He has now come to live in your heart, He will want to minister through you. There is so much to do for the Lord. Explore every avenue and ask God to help you find your niche. Some of the most fulfilled people I know are alone and single, but their lives are filled with the joy of living to the full for Jesus.

Commendation, which is approval, praise and appreciation, is the third vital building block in the healing of the family.

Tessie came to me with a serious alcohol and drug-dependency problem plus numerous inner conflicts. Her story illustrates the need for commendation in the family — and the devastating effect on the *whole* person who has not received it.

Two things she remembered from her childhood she related to me without emotion — she had come to accept them as part of her life because that's the way it was. When she was a small child, she made a card at school for her mother. She had worked so carefully on it, and she carried it home with great pride only to have her mother say, "Couldn't you do a better job than this? Look! It's smudged! What can I do with it?" and this mother tossed it aside. Tessie was crushed. She would never try again.

The second incident she remembered happened at school. Her work hadn't been up to par, and the teacher held her up to the ridicule of the whole class. In reporting this she said to me with almost hopeless indifference, "You see, I have always been a failure. It will never be any different."

But it was different when Jesus Christ healed Tessie. She was restored completely, and today is a self-assured and confident person.

We must learn to commend one another.

Parents — find something to appreciate in your child, something to commend him for. Then challenge him to reach his potential. I read the story of a lad whose job was to dry the supper dishes. One evening he dropped a very special dish and it lay in pieces on the floor. He flung down the dish towel, saying, "It's no use! I can never do anything right!" His mother was a Christian who had an open line to Heaven. Quickly she prayed for wisdom, then said, "Son, you've been drying dishes for me now for quite some time. This is the first time you've broken anything. I think that's something of a record." He looked up at her with a rather hesitant smile. Then he picked up the towel and said, "Yeah, you're right! It is a record, isn't it!" That's what I mean by commendation.

Husbands and wives — little things mean a lot. How long has it been, wife, since you said to hubby, "I sure appreciate you. I think you're the most wonderful guy I know. And I'm proud of you." Then watch him shine. And, hubby, give her a reason to feel this way, will you? Fix yourself up a bit, just for her. I wonder how long it has been since you said to her, "That was just the best dinner! Thanks a million!" Or — "Honey, you're beautiful. I really like that dress. I like the way you do your hair!" And, wife, please give him a reason to say this — like taking the curlers out of your hair and getting yourself gussied up a bit, just for him. You see, little things do mean a lot. Why not take a new look at one another. Find something good to commend in each other.

The family of God — don't be stingy with your praise and appreciation. Lots of lonely people are longing to be noticed, to have someone say a word of commendation and approval. Search them out and tell them so. Be liberal with smiles, courtesy, generosity.

A young man, tall and shy, stood before me after a meeting one night.

Embarrassed, hardly knowing what to say, he finally blurted out, "I just want you to know how much you have helped me. Here!" He was holding something behind his back, and as he said this, he handed me a package — from the florist. It looked as though he had sat on it all through the meeting! Then just before he was gone he said, "Oh, here's some stuff to put in the water so they will last." He gave me a small envelope, then disappeared into the crowd. I carried the package home, and when I opened it, I found six of the most beautiful red roses as fresh and beautiful as when he had bought them. They lasted a whole week. I have never met that young man since. I don't even know his name. But if he ever reads this book, I want him to know he made my day.

Teens and young people — how long has it been since you told Mom and Dad how much you appreciate them? Do you jump up from the table and go rushing off, or do you say "Thanks," to Mom and give her a little hug? No, you're not too big for that. Do you take Dad for granted with the attitude, "He's good for a buck when I need it." How long since you looked at him with pride and respect — and let him know it?

Another young man came to me after a seminar and said, "You know, I don't think I have ever told my mother that I love her. She is away right now, but as soon as she comes home that's the first thing I'm going to do!"
Commendation and appreciation bring healing into the family.

Compassion — The fourth building block in healing in the family is love in action. It is seeing another's need and doing something about it. Let us look at the compassion of Jesus in the Scriptures:

"Jesus was moved with compassion and He healed their sick" (Matt. 14:14).
"Jesus, moved with compassion, touched the leper and healed him" (Mark 1:41).
"Jesus...moved with compassion...fed the multitude" (Mark 6:34, 42).
"God, being full of compassion, forgave..." (Psalm 78:38).

Compassion is a "moving" thing. Some time ago when I realized how little of the love of Jesus flowed through my life, I asked the Lord to show me the meaning of compassion. The answer came in a way I hadn't expected. I was on the ferry which plies the waters between Vancouver and Vancouver Island — on my way to speak at a ladies' supper meeting. I had been very busy with not much time for preparation, and I was looking forward to the two-hour ferry trip to give me time to collect my thoughts and get my notes in order. I hadn't been seated very long in a quiet corner before I noticed some activity just across the aisle from me.

Turning around I saw a young girl, just a teenager, poorly dressed and a big knapsack on the seat beside her. Playing on the floor was a little baby chewing on an ashtray the mother had given her. She was about six months old, dressed only in a diaper. Running around nearby was a little girl, possibly five years old, dressed in oversize clothes. I found the situation most distasteful and turned quickly back to my notes on my lap. It wasn't a pleasant sight.

Then a Voice I knew so well spoke into my heart. "What are you going to do about it?"

"Lord, what could I possibly do?" I asked. "Furthermore, I must get these notes ready for this banquet." So I read the same two or three lines a few more times.

Then once again He said, "What are you going to do about it?"

"Lord, what can I do?" I replied. "They are so dirty, and I have on my new white suit." I am not proud of that response and shudder now to think that it's a wonder God didn't turn away from me at that moment. But do you know what He did? He simply said, "What are you going to do about it?"

This time I said, "Lord, show me what to do and I'll do it." Getting up from my seat, I walked over to the little mother and her children. By this time she was nursing the baby, and all she had on was a man's shirt. I didn't know what I was going to say. But sitting down beside her, I asked, "Would you like me to get you a cup of coffee and maybe a sandwich? And would the little girl like some milk?"

"Would you really?" she asked in amazement. The little girl seemed rooted to the spot. Finally she burst out with: "I thought I saw an angel!" (God and I knew this lady dressed in white was no angel!)

I went to the cafeteria and brought back a tray with some food, milk and coffee. The mother gave a biscuit to the baby and was trying to hold her and balance her coffee at the same time. Before I realized what I was doing, I had reached out and taken the baby in my arms. Gooey cookie ran down my white suit, but I didn't even care because Jesus was whispering to me, "This is what I mean by compassion."

Then I told them about the Lord and how dearly He loves them. She told me her name was Red, the baby's name was Boo, and the little girl's name was Nickie — that's all. I never saw her again, but I know she learned about the love of Jesus that day, and I learned about compassion. (And by the way, my suit sponged off in the washroom, and I didn't even need my notes to minister at that banquet.)

Compassion is *non-judgmental*. It protects from the critical eyes of the curious or the gossipers. It is *loyal*. It never tears down in front of others. It does not cast innuendoes nor subtle criticisms when the other is defenseless. It does not hold up to the public eye the faults and failings which we slip into so easily at home in unguarded moments. Compassion is rather the love which the Bible says "covers a multitude of sins" (I Peter 4:8.) It is the love which helps the other to overcome but never knocks him down. It heals in family, in the home and in the church.

Compassion is the love which does not demand a change — it produces one. It is that intangible something within us placed there by the Holy Spirit (Romans 5:5), wrought in us through the implanted Word. People can sense this compassion even though we may not be aware of them or even say a word.

I give the following illustration only for the glory of my Lord — and with a little hesitation — because I do not want anyone to misunderstand my motive. I am no different than any other Christian who walks with Jesus in the fulness of the Spirit. I was to speak at a luncheon some distance away and managed to arrive late because I took the wrong exit off the freeway. The ladies were already seated, so I was ushered immediately to the head table. As soon as I sat down, a woman rose from her place and walked through the crowd to stand by me. As I looked up at her, tears filled her eyes and she said, "What is it about you? When you walked by my table, I felt love for the first time in my life."

I had no special feeling at all, but a light bulb only has to stay plugged in and turned on in order to shine. This was the love of Jesus in an "earthen vessel". That woman found Jesus Christ as her Saviour that day.

Compassion is the love which is willing to forget itself and stick out its neck for the other person. Can you see that if each one of us saw the other person's need before our own, no one could lose? It means that when hubby comes home hot and tired from the job and I have had a hard day with the kids and everything has gone wrong, I don't immediately blast him with my troubles. I minister to him and love him.

God taught me a valuable lesson through a poodle. He talked to Baalim in the Old Testament through a donkey, but He used a poodle with me. When our kids were married, they decided Mom and Dad might be lonely, so they presented us with this one pound ball of white fluff. I said, "What on earth is it?" Our son replied, "It's a toy poodle. He'll need lots of love, and you'll have to give him a name."

Well, I didn't feel any need for such an animal — and where would I find a name? I said, "He sure doesn't look like a 'Pierre' to me." Just then the little dog got up on his feet, and he had the dearest little pom pom tail, so we called him "Pom Pom". He became a part of the family and dearly loved my husband. Pom Pom would sit at the window watching for Lloyd's truck to appear on the road. Then he would rush frantically to the back door to get out. Rushing down the driveway, he would hurl himself against Lloyd who would scoop him up in his arms. Then that poodle would lick him all over his face and neck while I'd stand at the window looking out at this display — and not too happy about it all.

One day when my husband came in I said, "That poodle sure gets a lot more loving than I do!"

"Well," Lloyd responded, "maybe if you went after it like the poodle...!"

The next day came. No, I didn't run down the driveway, but I didn't let Pom Pom out. And I beat him to the door! And I discovered that evening that it was really my arms my husband wanted around him — and my loving welcome, not the poodle's. I am so glad God taught me that lesson. It has made a great difference in our marriage.

Love is the great blender of personalities. In fact — LOVE IS THE GREATEST!

LOVE IS THE GREATEST!

*   *   *

"Now unto Him that is able to keep you from falling, and to present you faultless before the presence of His glory with exceeding joy, To the only wise God our Saviour, be glory and majesty, dominion and power, both now and ever. Amen" (Jude 24-25).